'Matt (and his show) are youthful in accessible but still insightful, informal things should be entertaining and Mat
MICHAEL JORDAAN, CEO

'*The Matt Brown Show* is an inspiration for entrepreneurs who want to learn from the giants that have come before them. Matt's shows are insightful and a good learning opportunity for startup and scale-up entrepreneurs.'
CLIVE BUTKOW, CEO of Kalon Venture Partners

'In the clutter that is the Internet, *The Matt Brown Show* is a crisp, fresh and alternative perspective that gives relief from all the clichéd content out there.'
ALLON RAIZ, Chief Excitement Officer of Raizcorp

'Laid back and high energy in combination – it's a formula that works. *The Matt Brown Show* connects innovators to the world.'
ZAPIRO

'*The Matt Brown Show* is a crazy galaxy of ideas that smash up normal conventions of business and society.'
BRIAN ALTRICHE, Founder and CEO of RocoMamas

'*The Matt Brown Show* has eaten its own dog food by taking the unique stories of African entrepreneurs to the global stage. It has left an inspiring legacy for many young entrepreneurs to aspire to.'
KEET VAN ZYL, Co-Founder and Partner of Knife Capital

'Matt Brown has built an extraordinary resource for entrepreneurs with *The Matt Brown Show*. His creativity, curiosity and tenacity have created a treasure trove of business knowledge that is always fun to listen to.'
HOWARD MANN, Founder of The Business Brickyard (New York) and Author of *Your Business Brickyard*

i

'Matt's approach is completely different to your average host; the result is that he can extract information that goes beyond the average I-have-heard-this-a-million-times-before answer. Mind-blowing stuff.'

MARNUS BROODRYK, *Shark Tank* Investor, Entrepreneur and Author of *90 Rules for Entrepreneurs*

'Matt Brown is Africa's answer to Tim Ferriss.'

RICHARD MULHOLLAND, Founder of Missing Link, Author of *Legacide* and *Boredom Slayer*

'Matt Brown is a fun, fascinating, entrepreneurial leader. His experience, energy and enthusiasm are infectious. Matt's insights and experience are super valuable for anyone who wants to design and build businesses.'

CHRISTOPHER LOCHHEAD, #1 Amazon Best-selling Author

'As these stories and case studies demonstrate, Matt has a nose for the unconventional. Where else could I be encouraged to attack a pile of analgesics with a baseball bat? Read on ...'

ANDY RICE, Speaker, Writer and Strategist

'Most shows are a straight-forward interview format: ask a question, provide an answer. *The Matt Brown Show* is a welcome change to that. An engaging one-on-one experience made all the more entertaining because Matt's team is part of the audience. *The Matt Brown Show*: It's fun. It's different. It works.'

GAVIN MOFFAT, Author of *Swimming with Sharks*

'*The Matt Brown Show* is one of those rare places today where proper conversations between actual human beings are still had, where ideas are given the time and space to develop into IDEAS. (And it's funny too).'

BRONWYN RUTH WILLIAMS, Trend Analyst and Futurist at Flux Trends

'*The Matt Brown Show* is one on which I could really be myself, dig into real issues and have fun. Matt's a good listener, and he, and the team, work hard on the inner as much as the outer. It's a winning combination.'

ROBIN WHEELER, Author of *Death is the Ultimate Orgasm*

'*The Matt Brown Show* is the perfect mix of entertainment, deep conversation, thought-provoking content and funky quirks. Matt has an innate ability, as host, to enable his interviewees to shine at their best.'

RICHARD WRIGHT, Renowned Speaker, Endurance Athlete and brain cancer survivor

'I truly enjoyed being interviewed on *The Matt Brown Show*; the whole process was professionally orchestrated. Matt's line of questioning was on point and the level of consistency speaks to a true professional at work. Matt is a powerful and dynamic entrepreneur.'

TANYA KUNZE, CEO of Swift Coaching

'Really enjoyed being on *The Matt Brown Show*. Had lots of fun while discussing some serious business issues.'

IAN FUHR, Founder of Sorbet

'Matt, your unique, say-it-as-it-is, jovial demeanour was professional, down-to-earth and truly energising during our interview.'

RUSTY LABUSCHAGNE, Author of *Beating Chains*

'I hadn't ever listened to a podcast when Matt Brown called me to talk KasiNomics. Now I'm hooked on podcasts, especially Matt's. His casual but inquisitive style, humour and engaging well-researched questions combine the hour flying by and ending too quick.'

GG ALCOCK, Author of *Third World Child*, *KasiNomics* and *KasiNomic Revolution*

'Matt Brown asks questions that really matter to people. His approach is personal and passionate and his message is powerful.'

LAUREN WOOLF, Founder of Mrs Woolf

'What a great two hours with Matt. Fun, vibey, sometimes challenging and an opportunity to really be myself. Loved it.'
CAROLINE RAVENHALL, Speaker and Human Performance Specialist

'*The Matt Brown Show* is all about learning the rules like a pro and then smashing them to create your own. He has grown one of South Africa's most favourite podcasts and takes his audience into a wonderland of imagination as he uses the art of storytelling to give his audience an exciting learning journey of success and failures with the crème de la crème in business. This guy is on fire!'
CARMEN MURRAY, Founder of Boo-Yah! and Host of *The Carmen Murray Show*

'I loved being interviewed by Matt! His infectious curiosity and wisdom makes for a sizzling interview.'
JUSTIN COHEN, Best-selling Author and International Speaker

'*The Matt Brown Show* celebrates all forms of entrepreneurship, so that we can gain knowledge from far and wide and apply it to our daily lives.'
CATHY DAVIES, Host of *Outpatients*, FOX Life

'It's not difficult to see why *The Matt Brown Show* is complete gold. The easy, conversational style of interviewing that Matt has brings out the best in you as a guest and engages you as a listener. I am a complete fan of Matt and the value he brings to the world through all that he does.'
CANDICE MAMA, Motivator, Coach and Kindness Activist

'Matt Brown has a unique talent for getting really smart people to share a lot of their intellectual magic in a cool and fun way. Meaningful, impactful and relevant doses of thinking that never disappoints!'
BRAD SHORKEND, Co-Author of *We Are Still Human*

'Matt shares his "Matt Brown Magic" in thoughtful, meaningful and accessible ways, leaving everyone who engages with him smarter. Matt is one heck of a clever guy with the spunk and character to build and do great things.'

ANDY GOLDING, Co-Author of *We Are Still Human*

YOUR INNER GAME

YOUR INNER GAME

12 Principles for High-Impact Entrepreneurs

MATT BROWN

TRACEY McDONALD PUBLISHERS

First published by Tracey McDonald Publishers, 2019
Suite No. 53, Private Bag X903, Bryanston, South Africa, 2021
www.traceymcdonaldpublishers.com

ISBN 978-0-6399558-0-3

Editing by Nadine Todd
Text design and typesetting by Patricia Crain, Empressa
Cover design by Maveshan Chetty
Cover compilation by Patricia Crain, Empressa

Printed by **novus print**, a division of Novus Holdings

For Franklin, Raegan and Nina Brown: May this book inspire you as much as you inspire me.

CONTENTS

INTRODUCTION

A CODE TO LIVE BY

There's no blueprint that guides entrepreneurs when they begin their journey. You have to draw on the experiences of mentors, business books, biographies and websites. Unfortunately, this will only get you so far. The rest comes down to experience.

Many of the most successful entrepreneurs in the world, and pretty much all of the entrepreneurs I have interviewed, do not have a degree. There is no such thing as a PhD in entrepreneurship. MBAs are great if your ambition is to work in the corporate space, suffer the burden of student debt and then compete with thousands of other MBA graduates all vying for the same job.

But in the world of entrepreneurship, to achieve success you need a 'QBE' or 'qualified by experience'. The problem is that life's too short for you to make all of your own mistakes. Trust me, I know – been there, done that, and it only leads to failure, both personally and financially.

I spent years going it alone until I learned the single most important lesson of entrepreneurship: To learn from the mistakes of others and to understand the principles that high-performance human beings live by is the key to your own success – whatever that success means to you.

After interviewing hundreds of successful entrepreneurs, authors and CEOs, it's clear that the thing that ties them all together is the set of principles that they apply in their model of the world. These principles combine to create a code that governs how they make decisions, and which propels them through seemingly unthinkable and insurmountable challenges in both their personal and business lives.

I call that code **Inner Game**. It activates an unbreakable character and supports the ability to persevere through any challenge. It unleashes the true potential of one's highest self. Inner Game determines whether you will put a dent in the universe or whether the universe will put a dent in you.

I have written this book to share the most inspirational qualities of ordinary people doing extraordinary things and I hope that by reading these stories they will inspire you to think big and dream even bigger. From a set of stories recounted to me on my podcast, I have outlined various principles that I believe form the foundation of highly successful entrepreneurs and human beings, anywhere in the world.

If you are reading this book, I want to say two things. First, thank you. I never dreamed that writing a book like this would be possible. To this day, I'm humbled to have the opportunity to make a difference through storytelling. My 'why' is the same today as it was when I started *The Matt Brown Show* in 2015: To help entrepreneurs succeed through information sharing at scale.

If I can inspire just one hopeful entrepreneur to back themselves and start a business, I've already achieved my goal. So, thank you for giving me the gift of your time to share these stories with you.

The second point I have to mention is that for a long time I didn't believe in myself. When I launched my first business in my early twenties I was young and arrogant. The world – and business – had some harsh lessons to teach me. I had failures and successes, but the successes didn't stick as much as the failures did. They impacted my view of the world and myself. I didn't give up, but my confidence was shaken.

And then I launched *The Matt Brown Show*. Through the interviews on my podcast I began to transform what I thought of myself. I met incredible people who showed me what's possible when you put your mind to it. We're all capable of great things. We just need to believe in ourselves and push on when we want to give up.

So, I believe in you, even if you don't believe in yourself right now. As entrepreneurs, we all go through this cycle of inner fear and doubt, regardless of how big a business we build. Believe me – I've interviewed entrepreneurs who have shot the lights out and redefined industries, and they've all experienced this.

What's important though is that we are always becoming something better than we were the day before. That's what this book is about – the becoming of one's true self by embracing the most uncertain of paths: entrepreneurship. If you leave with only one key takeaway when you've finished this book, I hope it's this: that you can enjoy the beauty of becoming, because when nothing is certain, anything is possible.

PREFACE

BECOMING AN ENTREPRENEUR

It was Cape Town in the early 1990s. South Africa was in the grip of apartheid and civil unrest was growing, with tensions heightened by the ever-increasing prospect of civil war. At the time my dad and his two business partners owned a gun shop, Cape Handgun, a single store in the basement of a run-down shopping centre in Adderley Street, in the centre of downtown. I can still recall the distinct smell of discharged gun powder from the indoor shooting range, which was always full.

As a seasoned entrepreneur, my father had been savvy enough to spot a gap in the market for a firearms reseller and that gap exploded in April 1993. Chris Hani, the chief of staff of uMkhonto weSizwe, the armed wing of the African National Congress (ANC) was assassinated outside his home in Dawn Park, Johannesburg. This kicked off a series of violent riots and protests across the country. South Africa was on the brink of an all-out civil war and civilians raced to buy guns. A lot of guns. Cape Handgun took hundreds of thousands in cash over the counter every single day. But less than two years later, the business was bankrupt.

As a 14-year-old boy, I couldn't understand how such a successful business could lose everything in such a short period of time. The store was always full of people – always. It wasn't until I began building businesses of my own that

I started to see what had happened. It wasn't that people were not buying guns anymore – they most definitely were. The business was profitable, it had loyal customers and it enjoyed a market that was readily consuming the products it was selling. On paper it should have been a success.

Except that it wasn't. Cape Handgun went bankrupt because the business model didn't lend itself to scale. You see, even though the store was profitable, to expand the business into another location would have required significantly more capital than was readily available to the owners. It could only grow so big.

But the most important reason why the business went under was because, what I like to call the 'Inner Game' code and principles that my dad and his partners used, created a paradigm of thinking about the business as one that couldn't scale beyond a single store. The business had grown to meet their desired level of success at that time and so the hunger for more growth dried up. Two years later, after Nelson Mandela's release from prison, the market moved in a direction they did not anticipate, sales slowed and Cape Handgun eventually went under. They couldn't recover because their vision for the business couldn't adjust to a shifting market.

What I didn't know at the time was that the highs and lows of that entire experience, watching my dad's success and then the business failure, would be the spark of my own entrepreneurial journey and the beginning of the discovery of a set of principles and codes that would change my life forever.

Over the years, hundreds of podcasts and nine businesses later, I've solidified the core precepts necessary for an 'Inner Game' that leads to happiness, success and leading a meaningful life filled with purpose.

Startup number one fed straight into my passions and since I can remember, those were business and music. In 1999 I was able to combine them, launching a record label called Voodoo Vinyl based in London. I focused primarily on the production and distribution of electronic dance music. Back then, if you were a record label you were in the business of moving vinyl. It was tried and tested, but it was also expensive. Test pressings, essentially an LP that was printed on acetate before your main production run to test the quality of the sound, cost a staggering £500 for a single record. To do a print run of 500 records would then set you back around £2 500 (£5 per record), with the hope that you could then sell each record at £10 a pop – a 50% margin (excluding your licensing and marketing costs).

If you didn't have a 'hit record', it was a tough business to be in. It was Cape Handgun all over again. Absolutely everything in the business *didn't* lend itself to scale, from the production of the records, to the way they were distributed, to the punters in the record shops.

What I did have going for me though, which my dad and his partners didn't, was a curiosity beyond my immediate market, and a willingness to change, not only my business model, but my Inner Game code too.

The dot-com boom was well underway. iTunes didn't exist and the music industry was still uncertain about what this 'Internet' thing was all about. A lot of industries missed the huge disruption that was heading their way – in my opinion, a lot of industries still are, two decades down the line.

I've been curious about the Internet ever since the day I installed a dial-up 56k modem with a software kit on compact disc (CD) from America Online (AOL). Once I connected to the Internet for the first time, my entire way of thinking around how to sell music to consumers shifted. If I could sell music online, direct to the consumer, my business suddenly became scalable. It changed everything. And I really wanted to scale. I wanted to be big. I was 20 years old and I was ready to take over the world.

But, like so many industries, the music industry wasn't ready for this paradigm shift in music consumption. It wasn't a big label that made the first inroads in this space; it was an Internet-based technology startup called Napster, which allowed people anywhere in the world to easily share their MP3 files with other participants.

In the blink of an eye, people were consuming and sharing music online – and at scale. Napster caused such a stink that the regulators eventually came and shut it down in 2001, some two years before iTunes was launched by Apple. But during this short period of time, a decades-old industry had fundamentally changed forever. By the time iTunes launched, I had also changed my thinking around Voodoo Vinyl and had redesigned and repositioned the business as an online music retailer. I was highly motivated to find a solution to my scale problem.

My approach was simple. Scale the business as quickly as possible using the Internet and avoid paying the exorbitant manufacturing costs of traditional vinyl. I needed to take everything digital and I needed to be quick. New players like Beatport.com in the US and Trackitdown.net in the UK were already launching their online stores. Everyone who had spotted the gap needed to be a part of this next evolution of music consumerism, but to do that, we needed a platform of some kind: A reason for any aspiring electronic music artist to connect and do business with us.

My solution was launching the Voodoo Vinyl Remix Network (VVRN) – an online forum that allowed any artist from anywhere in the world with an Internet connection to submit their original music for a remix by independent artists from anywhere else in the world. Artists would then tender their remixes in a predefined time period, with the winning remixes selected for digital release around the world on our label. We zeroed in on remixes for our platform for two reasons. First, artists who were making remixes tended to be younger and more comfortable and familiar with the Internet and tech and, so, they were more likely to utilise the platform than more traditional musicians. Second, the popularity of remixes was exploding at the time.

As a concept remixes were nothing new, but there was a growing trend around the world for remixes to become even more popular on radio than the original songs of established artists. Some artists such as Björk, Nine Inch Nails and Public Enemy embraced this trend and outspokenly sanctioned fan-remixing of their work. The Grammys, the world's largest music awards ceremony, jumped onto the trend by announcing a 'Remixer of the Year' award for the first time in 1998. The award was won by Frankie Knuckles, widely regarded as 'the godfather' of electronic dance music, and many aspiring artists were suddenly trying to create hit remixes and become the next Frankie Knuckles. We had a platform that gave them access to a consumer market, and before we knew it, we'd cornered a niche that couldn't have been more relevant at that time in music history.

Four years after VVRN's launch, we had attracted artists and produced remixes for some of the industry's biggest names, including Boy George, The Human League, Tommy Boy Records (NY), Sony, Warner Music and EMI. At the height of VVRN's success in 2005, we were receiving 15 000 unique visitors a day on our remix network forum and we were releasing over 100 albums a year on vinyl and digital download through various distributors and our own online store.

The remix network was a novel idea that lent itself to scale through the Internet and it became the driving force behind the Voodoo Vinyl record label. I regarded the label as a success because it had scaled beyond what I had originally imagined, and I was most proud that we were providing a platform for unknown artists to break into new dance-related genres from anywhere in the world.

None of it would have been possible if my thinking around the business had not fundamentally shifted. If we remained a vinyl-only business, we would have gone bankrupt – the entire vinyl industry collapsed just two years after I pivoted the business.

After six years though, I had become tired of the music industry itself and with it my passion for the business-end. Competition was steadily increasing and I had a sense that it was the right time for a new challenge. After VVRN was sold, I made a mistake I now know many, many entrepreneurs make – particularly when they've experienced a measure of success. I started operating under the (mistaken) assumption that I knew what I was doing – particularly when it came to scaling a business.

I was young, I was arrogant, and I hadn't really failed in a major way as an entrepreneur. Luckily, the world was going to fix that for me. I was still based in London and my next venture was a self-help focused startup called Animus Potential ('Mind Potential'). I believed I could inspire people to create the life of their dreams. I developed as many relevant skills as I could and became a qualified hypnotherapist, a neuro-linguistic programming (NLP) practitioner and Time Line Therapist. I was on a mission to build a big business by 'helping one billion people in the next five years' – yes, that was my Big Hairy Audacious Goal (my BHAG, and I really, *really* believed in it).

There was just one small problem, which despite my best efforts, I could not overcome: Very few people want to take advice about life from a 26-year-old. All of a sudden, being an entrepreneur sucked in a very big way. You see, I was suffering from what my good friend Rich Mulholland calls 'entrepreneur belief'. A belief so powerful that it overwhelms all available logic and reasoning and often leads an entrepreneur to failure (typically when an entrepreneur first starts out). My thoughts about the business started to become suffocated and with that the business shrank from existence.

It was my first big failure and it was crushing. It made me question everything. What the hell did I know about business anyway? I was a world-class failure. I ended up booking two first-class tickets to the failure train. Any entrepreneur who has lost a business jumps onto that train. Some get off, and others never leave. Every *successful* entrepreneur I know has experienced this at one point or another. It's part of the process of building businesses. The difference is, they're in the group that gets off the train.

These business breakdowns are never the end if you're able to shift your thinking, because when you do, your breakdowns become your breakthroughs. I learned the hard way: the one thing that is fundamental to becoming a successful entrepreneur is **never giving up**. You get two types of entrepreneurs: Those who let their fear of failure define them, and those who let their fear of failure push them forward. If you're going to build anything of value, you need to decide right up-front which entrepreneur you're going to be and then stick to it. This way, if you lose the business, you don't lose the lesson. This is what *successful* entrepreneurship is all about.

The thing that got me off the failure train was a burning hunger to try again. Deep down, the idea of letting a moment of failure define me for the rest of my life was far scarier than the failure itself. I knew I could pick myself up and try again – I just had to stop feeling sorry for myself.

At the time, even though I'd managed to pull myself together, I wasn't ready for another entrepreneurial venture and I ended up working as a management consultant in London. Two years later, my love affair with entrepreneurship started up again when I moved to the South of France.

My goal was to work on superyachts – the playground of billionaires and the super-rich. A superyacht is the pinnacle of luxury and decadence. But more so, a personal yacht offers something you can't get with most large vessels: privacy. These yachts cost upwards of hundreds of millions of dollars and some are well over 100 metres (330 feet) in length. Standard superyacht features include helicopter pads, movie cinemas, swimming pools, Jacuzzis, music studios, tenders and some even have underwater torpedo systems to stave off any potential pirate attacks. Superyachts are the ultimate status symbol for the super-rich – far more desired than any supercar or hyper-car – but unless you're personal friends with a billionaire or a famous celebrity, actually getting onto these yachts isn't an easy thing to do.

Many aspiring superyacht crew members spend months walking the docks on both sides of the Atlantic looking for employment and most don't find it. The biggest challenge is that you need experience. If you don't have experience, even if you have the right qualifications, it's hard to break into the industry. But if you do, the world of a highly exclusive club, reserved for a very select few, opens up to you. You also make tax-free cash (and a lot of it too).

In 2008, there was precious little information available about how to crack your way into this highly exclusive industry. But there were many, many people who wanted to – a captive audience you might say. It wasn't unusual to see a line, hundreds of people long, outside a recruitment agency in Antibes, France, at the beginning of the season.

To shine a light on the industry, I launched a blog and started writing about my own experiences walking the docks of popular superyacht havens between Cannes in France, the Principality of Monaco and all the way to Livorno in Italy. After two months I managed to land a gig on a 50-metre yacht in Monaco and, once inducted into crewing, I kept writing.

My blog was full of helpful tips and tricks and provided readers with everything they needed to know about how to find work, how to get the right qualifications for specific roles and gave an inside look into the world of superyachts that inspired 'outsiders' to keep going. Within three months I had over 10 000 unique visitors a month. Industry magazines like *Dockwalk*, started picking up and publishing my content. Within six months, my blog had grown to 45 000 unique visitors a month from over 30 different countries. Once again, a simple and novel idea had scaled thanks to the Internet.

It was a crazy time. Everything was moving quickly and scaling beyond any of my original expectations. At one point, I was flown to Monaco in a private helicopter to write about the launch of new superyachts. After publishing my content in every edition of their magazine for over a year, *Dockwalk* eventually offered me a position as a full-time writer in Florida.

The growth I was experiencing was awesome. In some ways I was flying high. But it also came at a price. I wasn't particularly happy and deep down I knew I was going to leave the industry. I declined the opportunity with *Dockwalk* and instead decided to take all the content I had written and package it into a book called *The Dynamic Deckhand – The Definitive Guide to a Superyacht Crew Career*, which I released on my blog as an e.book. After four years gallivanting around the Mediterranean, Caribbean and the east coast of the United States, I started thinking about returning to South Africa and starting another business. I had no idea what that would be, but I was ready for some roots.

And then a different opportunity presented itself. It wasn't long after releasing my e.book that I received an email from Neil, an entrepreneur based in Birmingham. Neil had written a book called *Get a Cruise Ship Job* and suggested we explore a joint venture.

Neil and I met in London a month or so later and put together the foundations of an information product marketing business that would sell 'how to' advice on the Internet by way of dollar-based monthly subscriptions. Our approach was to deliver the content online in modular courses and market them using a mix of email and affiliate partnerships. We built a sizeable list of 80 000 subscribers by offering free guides in exchange for email addresses and used this database to market our courses online.

Initially, trying to figure out how to scale this business proved challenging. You can have the biggest list in the world, but if the demand for the thing that you are selling isn't there, or you get your launch strategy wrong, you'll just end up with lacklustre sales results.

During our first launch we didn't really know what we were doing. We spent six months building the content for the launch of a subscription site and at the end of the day we had only made a few thousand dollars. Realising that we had picked a niche that wasn't liquid enough, we started diversifying into other travel-related employment niches. This, combined with improving our internal product launch processes, meant the business soon struck gold. Within two years the business was making more than $100 000 in a single day from an online product launch. The entire idea, platform and delivery was a success.

It sounds like a dream come true. I'd learned a lot about online marketing systems and how they can be used to help automate sales. But there's a challenge with automating things too: Eventually, you *will* get bored. Or maybe I'm just built like that.

Either way, from my perspective, I felt that the business had reached a 'success plateau'. Like Voodoo Vinyl, I lost my passion for it. This is a pretty big deal. Building a successful business takes tremendous work, focus and dedication. Without passion, it's almost impossible to give the business what it needs. When I thought about the future, I stopped thinking big. I was thinking small and not doing the business any favours. I eventually sold my portion of the company to Neil and cashed out. Failure will always teach you more than success – a lot of success teaches you nothing – but I had learned something here. It's important not to get bored.

This time, it wasn't long before I founded my next startup, Kidmogo. Kidmogo was designed to solve a universal problem for parents around the world: Knowing where their kids are at all times. It was essentially a bracelet that allowed any parent to track the location of their child via a mobile app. I came up with the idea while researching GPS tracking devices for my car. I wasn't a parent at the time, but I could see there'd be a market for the product, and I pitched the idea to one of my closest family members, Mike Brown, a UK-based entrepreneur, and he decided to join me as co-founder of the business.

At first, we imported the product from a supplier in China, but after inspection fees and import duties the monthly cost to the customer was quite high and the product itself wasn't very durable – a big problem for very busy kids. We decided instead to design our own product, which we would manufacture locally in South Africa.

Neither of us had any background in GPS tracking devices or manufacturing, so we enlisted the help of electrical engineers and product designers. We spent hundreds of thousands, and seed capital, on the development of a new product that would allow us to go to market at a much more attractive price, but more importantly, our goal was to have a superior product to anything else currently available on the market (locally and internationally). Many months and 3D-printruns later, we realised that to get the business off the ground we needed to sink significantly more capital into the development of the product than we originally anticipated.

Unfortunately, with no product or customers, we couldn't raise the capital either, so like any startup without funding, it didn't see the light of day. At least, that was the story I repeatedly told myself: 'We couldn't raise funding, so the business failed.'

It was a nice little bullshit line I was feeding myself. The real reason it failed was because I quit. My Inner Game at the time dictated to me that I quit. I gave up when things got real and questions were asked of me that I either didn't have answers for, or didn't have the hunger to find answers for. Here's the truth: There is always another move. Always. We didn't even exhaust all available funding options. At the time, crowdfunding was already a well-established funding route, and yet we didn't even try it – and we had a product that we knew had universal appeal with parents around the world. If we had just scaled our thinking and refused to quit, Kidmogo could have been a very different business.

Kidmogo was another failure notch on my belt, and once again I turned to the corporate world while I tried to figure things out. I was attracted to the idea of how creative agencies approached scale-thinking when it came to building the world's biggest brands. As a result, I spent several years working inside the world's largest and most creative agencies. Any entrepreneur can tell you that the itch doesn't go away – and I was certainly no exception – but I learned a lot during those years as well.

It took me a while to figure out my next entrepreneurial play, but when I did, it was an idea that drew on all of the experiences I'd had up to that point. By this stage, I was back in South Africa, married and a dad myself. My big idea was called *The Digital Kungfu Show* (later rebranded as *The Matt Brown Show*) – a podcast whose sole purpose was to help entrepreneurs around the world succeed through information sharing at scale.

In January 2015, one of the growing trends in the US was an audio-only medium called podcasting. In South Africa, podcasting wasn't popular at all. In fact, as an industry, it was almost non-existent. I wasn't a kid living in a flat in London anymore, or touring around the Mediterranean. I had real responsibilities. But you can't turn that entrepreneurial switch off. I've interviewed hundreds of entrepreneurs, and we recognise our own. You'll take that risk because you *need* to.

So, instead of staying in an agency and playing it safe, I took a big bet on an untested industry. Having worked with trends pretty much my entire adult life, I had a hunch that as smartphone penetration increased in South Africa, it would only be a matter of time before podcasting would catch on. To help launch the platform, I needed some prelaunch content and so I set up some initial interviews with thought leaders in the advertising and business space. I had no idea what I'd let myself in for.

In the early days of podcasting (well, *my* early days), I really, really sucked at it, for many reasons – I had barely even listened to a podcast, let alone produced one. Listeners of my show wouldn't guess it today, but I'm a natural intro-vert. I generally prefer to hang out with people I know and like, and I've been that way my entire life. Sitting down with a stranger and trying to hold a conversation with them for an hour wasn't just difficult, it was agonising. Like I said, I sucked at it. To this day, I'm not even sure how I got through those first few episodes.

The very first episode I released was an interview with the technology trends specialist Arthur Goldstuck. I uploaded it to iTunes and then expected the world to come and listen to it. I went to bed happy. I woke the next morning eager to see how many thousands of downloads I'd received and to my surprise, shock and terror I saw what no podcaster should ever see – just one single download (probably from me the day before when I was checking the audio).

I wasn't new to the digital space, or creating and marketing digital content. I'd had some pretty big successes in this space – hell, *all* of my successes up to that point had been in sharing online content in one form or another. What the hell was happening?

It was a gruelling first few weeks. I wish I could say the Arthur Goldstuck episode was an anomaly. It wasn't. After a few weeks I was wondering why I'd been dumb enough to start a podcast in the first place. The failure train was calling me to board again and I almost pulled the plug on the whole thing.

Here's what I now know: most podcasts, like businesses, don't survive past their first six months. I can barely count the number of times I've heard or spoken to entrepreneurs who say they are going to start a podcast, but then never do. Of the ones that do start podcasting, a very small percentage survives and there's a very good reason for that. For the most part, at least in the early days, it's hard, thankless work. You end up putting in a huge amount of effort for very little return. It was enough to get me thinking long and hard about quitting.

If I had quit, there would be no *Matt Brown Show* today. This book wouldn't exist. I'd probably be back in corporate, or working on another startup. So, what made quitting this time different to all the other times? I walked away from a number of businesses for very different reasons. I exited successful businesses because the passion was gone. I walked away from unsuccessful businesses because I wasn't willing to push through that incredibly painful barrier that most startups face at some point.

But with the podcast I pushed through, and I think it's because I'd had my fair share of quitting, and I'd learned from it. I was finally ready for my big play. When I was 26 and thinking about giving up on Animus Potential, I called Damien, a business coach I was friends with, and asked him if I should quit. He said to me: 'Matt, I won't tell you what to do, but I will tell you a story. There was once a military general who built a highly-skilled army. They sailed across the sea in a fleet of ships to invade a foreign land. The only problem was that the army of that foreign land was five times bigger than his own army. When the fleet eventually made land, the general instructed his lieutenants to burn all the ships.'

Being the young, arrogant shit that I was at that time, I replied: 'What the fuck has this got to do with me quitting my business?' I hung up the phone on him, irritated with what I saw as a completely irrelevant piece of advice. One week later, the business went under. But the story stuck with me and years later, on the brink of quitting another business, it bubbled up. This time, after years of experience – both good and bad – I suddenly got the lesson in a major way.

The general burned all those ships so that his army knew there was only one way forward. There was no return. Quitting was not an option. And, so, I made the decision to persist, week after week, month after month. I didn't focus on my lacklustre download numbers. I looked ahead.

I learned that sometimes, in order to build something of value, you need to focus on the small steps to build your foundations. I also discovered that sucking at something is the first step towards being sort of good at something. The more I sucked at it, the better at podcasting I became. Instead of scripting every interview down to the finest details, I started winging it. Instead of chasing big names for interviews, they started being referred to me and 18 months later I had built a loyal listenership in over 100 countries around the world without spending a cent on advertising.

Not giving up on *The Matt Brown Show* has given me an incredible gift as an entrepreneur: at the time of writing this book I was more than 150 episodes in. That's 150 interviews with incredible people, from entrepreneurs and authors to a Dakar finisher. Each one has taught me something valuable. My goal was to help entrepreneurs launch and build their businesses around the world through information sharing – real lessons and insights from people who have been there and done that.

If you're an entrepreneur (or want to be), I can guarantee you that at some point you will face tremendous adversity on your journey. There will be moments when you're swimming in a sea of entrepreneurial confidence and other moments when you will feel like you're going to drown in the heavy grip of fear, uncertainty and doubt.

There'll be defining moments when you'll either shrink under the dark clouds of scale or shine through and grow despite them. Ultimately, it's about how you interpret and deal with these pressures that matter. Because when it feels like your business won't survive another day, how you think about your business and your personal ability to push through will be the defining factor of whether you're able to push forward. It all starts with you, and your Inner Game as the entrepreneur. You don't have to do it alone. You can learn from those who have come before you, and be inspired by them.

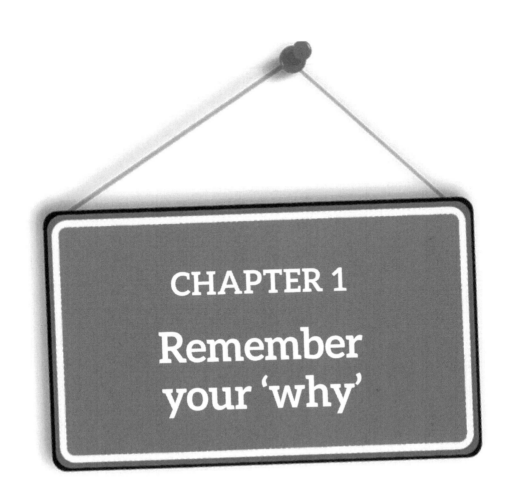

CHAPTER 1

Remember your 'why'

Player:	**Joey Evans**, Dakar Rally finisher, author and motivational speaker
Episode:	MBS097
Principle:	*I will remember my 'why'*

When you feel like quitting,
remember why you started.

– Anonymous

Joey Evans has always loved bikes, from his first second-hand Raleigh Strika at the age of six to the powerful off-road machines that became his passion later on in life. His dream was to one day ride the most gruelling off-road race in the world, the 9 000 kilometre Dakar Rally.

But on 13 October 2007, with two races left in a regional off-road racing championship and his highly competitive sights set on a win, Joey, who was determined to take the 'hole shot' (first corner) ahead of the field, crashed his bike at the start of the race and was ridden over by almost every bike competing that day. His back broken, Joey woke up spitting out his own shattered teeth and unable to feel his legs. He had crushed his T8 and T9 vertebrae and was paralysed from the chest down.

'It completely shattered my Dakar dream and my life as well. You spend years working towards a dream and then one day everything evaporates and the future you imagine for yourself is gone. Everything is gone,' he told me when I interviewed him.

The accident was completely devastating for Joey, his wife and their four daughters (all under the age of eight years old). 'The thought of not being able to play with them on the beach, teaching them to ride bicycles and not walking them down the aisle killed me.'

But Joey didn't give up. He's my ultimate example of Inner Game at work. Lying in his hospital bed, barely able to move, he decided to use his dream of competing in the Dakar Rally to help him overcome his physical impairments.

His first two doctors didn't believe he'd ever walk again, let alone compete in the world's toughest endurance rally, but the third wanted to fuse his back to take pressure off his spinal cord, and he offered some hope. Joey had an incomplete spinal cord injury, which meant the spinal cord was compressed, but not severed. In theory, this meant that when the swelling eventually went down, and with enough physical therapy, Joey might, potentially, one day get out of his wheelchair, although the doctor didn't know whether Joey would walk again.

This was the truth that Joey decided to make his own.

'Every day I woke up and had to make the decision to get up and work at my recovery,' says Joey. The problem was that most days there was nothing there to work with. He had no feeling in his legs and they were starting to waste away. 'That's when the reality would set in. I'd ask myself if this was how it was going to be for the rest of my life.'

Imagine your body refusing to do what your mind wants it to do. Imagine the desperation, the frustration, the terror. *And you wake up every morning, day after day, and keep trying anyway.*

After his back-fusion surgery, Joey was hoping for a miracle, but it didn't result in the change in fortunes he was hoping for. As each day and week passed optimism slipped further away and Joey found himself in a place of darkness and hopelessness. He got up each day anyway. He pushed on. Even though he was no longer sure why, he still wasn't ready to give up.

And then one day, he felt a little twitch in his right big toe. Despite incredible pain, he began to work that toe every day, over and over again. If Joey believes in anything, it's the old sporting mantra of, 'No pain, no gain'. As the weeks wore on, he eventually regained feeling in his ankle, which slowly expanded into his right quad muscle and then the rest of his body.

'Even though I couldn't move the muscle, I could feel that something was there. I did the only thing that made sense – I worked the muscle. I'd count repetitions until the muscle would fatigue and I couldn't feel anything, and then I'd rest. Once the muscle recovered, I'd begin again.' Joey was able to stand with support three months later, and shortly after that began walking again.

In many ways, Joey's recovery is a miracle, but some things can never be changed. He'll never be the way he was pre-accident. Twelve years later, he doesn't have 100% feeling in his legs, he can't feel hot or cold, he can't jump, his feet have permanent pins and needles, and he will always have bowel-control issues.

'These problems are my reality. I'll be dealing with them for the rest of my life. There are a lot of other complications that might affect how long I will live as well. All things considered, it's pretty grim,' he says. 'And one part of me believes that I have every right to feel freakin' miserable about my life because this is the reality I live in. But here's the thing: I can walk. I can ride a bike. I can go watch my kids play hockey and I can walk my daughters down the aisle one day. I can do cool stuff. And I choose to focus on that and the difference I can make to the people around me, and because of that I've been able to achieve the things I've always wanted to achieve.'

THE POWER OF CHOICE

Positive thinking isn't about always expecting the best to happen. It's about accepting that whatever happens is the best thing for this moment in time. Joey believes this simple mindset made all the difference in his recovery.

'I've seen people who have lived full, awesome lives after an injury like this and I've seen people who have lived miserable, horrible lives and in both categories there are people who walk again and people who don't walk again. I realised I had a choice to make. You don't get to choose if you're going to live in a wheelchair or not, but you do get to choose if you're going to live a full, happy life or not. There are guys out there who have to live with catheters for their entire lives and they can bitch and moan about how tough that is and will choose to be miserable. But then there are guys who are stuck in a wheelchair who would kill for the opportunity to be in their position. Either way, it's your choice to become who you want to be and how you will live your life.'

Practising the art of gratitude helped Joey to keep going when things got really tough. 'When I was in hospital, I looked at the injuries of patients around me, and I took stock of my life and choices. One woman slipped in the shower, broke her back and will never walk again. There was a man who was hit by a drunk driver and whose head injury is so bad he doesn't recognise his wife. Another patient is now a quadriplegic – he has lost all feeling and movement below his neck. He will never be able to use his hands, pick up a phone, hold his wife's hand or touch his child's face.

'I was racing dirt bikes and that came with risks – I rolled the dice, the six came up, I got nailed, and I had to accept that. I could wallow, or recognise how much I still had. Even in a wheelchair I could still do a lot. I realised that I didn't want my wife and kids to suffer. My attitude, and how I faced this new reality, would play a large part in how they faced our new reality as a family.

'You can let yourself go sometimes; it's what you do next that counts. Gratitude is a muscle. The more you work it, the stronger it becomes, and the higher the probability that you will be able to pick yourself back up and keep going when everything seems hopeless.'

Two years later, Joey was back on a bike, chasing his goal of competing in the Dakar. At first it was a disaster – he had no core muscles, and if the bike fell, he couldn't get back up. But he pushed himself and four years after the accident he was back on a race track. Which was when a whole new reality set in.

'I'm competitive and I've always had a natural talent for sports. I was captain of the team, I did ultramarathons, I wanted to win. And now I was hacking it out at the back of the field, getting lapped by every other racer on the track.'

It's during times of adversity that we truly realise what we're made of. Talent got Joey to where he was before his accident. Resilience got him to where he is today – and it was a humbling experience.

'When the mind and body don't align, you end up on a self-reflective journey. I was working harder than I ever had before and I just kept falling over and getting lapped. I wanted to scream, "This isn't me, I'm not this guy". Except that I was that guy. I was last. Stone last. But I was there. And I wasn't giving up.

'There are physical and mental elements to recovery and in both cases it's about getting back up when you fall. Getting out of the chair, I learned to recognise when dark days were closing in so that I could pull myself back out. Physically, I learned that I was only competing with myself. That was all that mattered. Are you doing the best you can do? Are you putting everything you have into your dreams and goals? And are you getting back up when you fall down? I had to learn to stop worrying about the rest of the field and concentrate on myself and achieving my goals. That first race, I just wanted to complete one lap. That's all I focused on.'

Six years after his accident, Joey was finishing races and competing in multiple day races. His Dakar goal was finally in sight again. And then one day he was racing along the Mozambique border in the Pongola 500, and in a split second a cow ran out in front of Joey's bike and he T-boned it.

Three hours later, medivacked to a hospital in Richards Bay, his collarbone separated from his shoulder, a broken elbow, his triceps torn off his elbow, two broken ribs and a ripped open forearm, exposing the bone – Joey was a mess.

After six long years of never giving up, even when the darkness threatened to close in, of learning how to walk again, ride a bike again and finish endurance races, hitting a cow (of all things) sends a pretty clear message. You have to wonder what you did wrong in a previous life.

Joey was in hospital for another six months. And he still wasn't ready to give up. Several surgeries later, the goal of finishing the Dakar was burning strong, but he had started to wonder what price he'd have to pay to make his dream a reality. It had already cost him so much. Would it eventually cost him his life?

I asked Joey what his one piece of advice would be to give entrepreneurs the perspective shift they need to keep pushing in the face of enormous adversity. 'You have to see the goal, I mean *really* see it, and realise where you want to be,' he said. 'If it's worthwhile, then everything else is just the details. It doesn't matter how many times you hit a cow. Nothing worth doing is easy. You have to ask yourself: Am I tough enough to do this or am I going to tap out right now?'

This same sentiment has come through from several interviews on my podcast, even if the circumstances are different. The lesson is simple though: **don't give up**. Visualise your success and then go for it – no matter what.

CONQUERING THE DAKAR

The Dakar Rally spans almost 9 000 kilometres (5 592 miles) over 13 days across some of the world's toughest terrain. That is equivalent of riding from Cape Town, South Africa to Cairo in Egypt plus another 1 000 kilometres (652 miles). To make matters more exciting, over the course of the Dakar's 39 years, there have been 70 fatalities. This is the toughest off-road race in the world and for very good reason.

You can't just decide one day that you're going to compete in the Dakar. It's not a race you simply enter. You have to be accepted by the race organisers. In order to participate, potential competitors submit their CVs, detailing all the races they've competed in, as well as at least one international rally.

Joey bought himself a place on a French racing outfit so that he could compete internationally. After completing a six-day rally in the Sahara Desert and Morocco, he had the necessary international experience, and he could finally submit his entry and his CV. He then waited six weeks for an email response from the organising committee. When the response finally arrived, it was good news. He'd been accepted to compete in the 2017 Dakar Rally. Which was just the beginning of Joey's problems. This was where things got really complicated.

There are two ways to compete in the Dakar. You can be a professional racer and a paid member of a team, or you can enter as a privateer and pay your own way. It costs around $100 000 (R1,5 million) as a privateer, and it's incredibly hard work because you don't have a full support crew. Joey secured a spot on a Dutch team, but he still needed to raise R1,1 million to get to the Dakar.

Joey didn't have a large corporate sponsor. Instead, he had to convince hundreds of ordinary people to open their hearts and their wallets. Every sponsor's name is on his Dakar bike – homage to how everything we achieve in life is ultimately a group effort. But first he had to give them a reason to believe in him.

'I've learned that if you give people a cause and say "join me", they'll do it. But someone has to start. I had to say, "This is my dream, and I'm going", and then sponsors came on board. If you share your vision, it's incredible how people will support you.'

Joey's real challenge was sharing his story. Until that point, only people close to him knew what he'd been through. Now, he had to be vulnerable and let other people in. 'My story was covered far and wide. I had so many eyes on me. You can crumble under that kind of pressure, or you can use it to drive you – again, it comes down to a choice. It taught me there are so many different forms of courage.'

As a family, Joey, his wife and their four daughters went out to raise the money he needed to follow his dream. It took them six months. 'We had donations ranging from R50 to R100 000, but we reached our goal. It's just money after all.'

On 2 January 2017, Joey was lined up at the start line of the Dakar with two other countrymen. At that point, in the entire history of the Dakar Rally, only nine South Africans had ever completed the race on a bike. Joey knew his chances of finishing were incredibly slim. Over half the competitors at the start line don't finish the race. But he was there, and that was what counted. Of course, we've already seen Joey's fighting spirit at work. He knew his chances were slim, but he was going to give it his all anyway.

At the end of day five, out of the three South Africans who had started the Rally, only Joey was still in the race. Walter Terblanche's motor burned out while at high altitudes in the dunes and David Thomas had a massive high-speed crash, breaking his leg in numerous places. He had to be medivacked out of the race in a helicopter (Joey actually helped put him into the chopper).

Joey was still in the race, but things were looking grim. He'd torn the ligaments on the inside of his knee and it didn't look like he'd be able to keep going. 'Not being able to feel pain in certain parts of my body actually turned out to be a good thing,' he jokes. Joey was advised by the medics to retire from the race but instead of agreeing with them, he had a little pep talk with himself instead. '"You didn't come this far, to only come this far." That's what I kept telling myself. It had taken me ten years to get to that start line. I just had to hack it out for two weeks. That's it. I convinced myself I could do anything for two weeks.' So, the medics strapped up his knee and off he went.

On the second last day, at 10 am in the desert of Argentina, Joey was run over by another competitor driving a car. To this day, Joey doesn't know which competitor hit him. Thanks to a detection system fitted onto each competitor's bike or vehicle, he knew a car was coming up behind him, and so he was able to throw himself out of the way, but his bike was almost completely destroyed. With some 660 kilometres (410 miles) still to go to the end of the stage, Joey thought he was finished. His dream was finally over.

All competitors have a button on their bikes, which if pushed will send a signal to the race organisers that you are out of the race. 'I decided before the start line on that first day that I would never push that button. I'd wait for the sweeper truck to come collect me at the end of the stage instead.'

This decision gave Joey time. He was stone last, but he also wasn't going anywhere. And so he began attempting to make his bike rideable. On his mangled bike, with only one foot peg and no exhaust, he began moving forward. Unable to ride in the rutted main track with the cars and trucks he rode in a zigzag fashion through the semi-desert terrain. For all intents and purpose, he was out of the race. And then the most remarkable thing happened. In the middle of the desert he found a KTM Rally Replica – the exact same bike that he was competing on. There was nobody there.

'I went up to the bike and at first it didn't dawn on me what was happening. And then I couldn't believe what I was seeing.' It turned out that a Colombian rider had crashed. He'd broken his arms, pushed his button and had been medivacked out of the race. His bike was left for the sweeper truck. The rules of the Dakar are clear: You have to finish each stage on your own bike. But there are no rules around which spare parts you put on that bike.

With the help of some local Argentinians, Joey began stripping the abandoned bike, using what he could to repair his own bike. Eventually, he got his bike working. He would later box all those parts up and send them back to their owner, thanking him for the chance to finish the Dakar. Joey then climbed back onto his cobbled-together bike and rode through the night to make the cut-off time of 4 am. At 2:11 am he arrived at the checkpoint. He was able to get one precious hour of sleep before climbing back onto his bike to ride another 700 kilometres (430 miles) to finish the Dakar Rally.

NOBLE EXCUSES

There were many justifiable reasons for Joey to quit. He spent six months in painful recovery after hitting a cow. No one would have faulted him for giving up on his Dakar dream. Raising R1,1 million is tough. No one would have looked down at him if he hadn't achieved that goal. He tore his ligaments, managed only a few hours of sleep each night during the race and finally got driven over by another car. Why didn't he just quit? No one – and I mean no one – would have thought any less of him. So, what kept him going?

When I asked him this question, his answer was so simple. 'I saw myself riding up that finisher's ramp and crossing the finishing line. I just kept envisioning the end, and that created a mindset that it had already happened. I had to go on.'

Joey believes this is an essential step towards achieving your goals. 'If you don't do this, you'll never make it. There were many ways for me to come home – I call them noble excuses. Everyone is going to pat you on the back and say "Good job Joey, you tried and that's what counts" but I knew that there was no reason good enough for me not to finish this race. There is always a reason to quit, so you have to find the reason *why* you are going to finish. My reason was to beat my injury. This was a fight I'd been fighting for ten years. I had to see it through.'

And so, Joey Evans, ten years after breaking his back and being told it was unlikely he'd ever walk again, became the tenth South African ever to finish the Dakar Rally on a motorcycle.

If you're in need of some inspiration then I highly recommend that you read the full story of Joey Evans in his book *From Para to Dakar*.

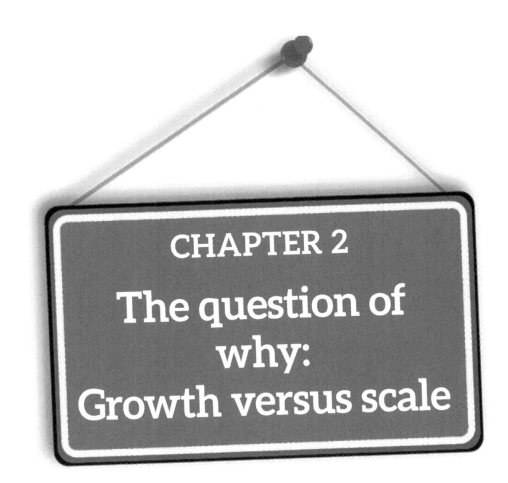

CHAPTER 2

The question of why:
Growth versus scale

Player:	**Joey Evans**, Dakar Rally finisher, author and motivational speaker
Episode:	MBS097
Principle:	*I will find my purpose*

When you're surrounded by people who share a passionate commitment around a common purpose, anything is possible.

– HOWARD SHULTZ

*J*oey's story isn't about an entrepreneurial dream, but his resilience is incredibly powerful, and my own journey has taught me how much resilience we need as entrepreneurs. Your why – your dreams, goals, and the difference you want to make – are what really matter if you want to achieve anything of noteworthy importance.

Often, when I ask young and aspiring entrepreneurs what they want out of life, they say 'success' and I get that. Every entrepreneur deserves to be successful and to build a business that can support the life of their dreams. But that can't be the full story because yes, you need to know what success looks like for you, but above all else, you need to know *why* you're aiming for that particular success. Why do you want to grow *that*? We all want to grow our businesses, but very few of us can answer the question, why? And to what end? Also, there is a big distinction between growth businesses and businesses that are scaling – they are very different animals, and if you can't differentiate between them, ultimate success and happiness, are unlikely.

A growth business is any business that generates positive cash flows or earnings, at the same or at a slightly faster rate than the overall economy. Typically, this is a business that operates with a handful of people in a single market and is based in one location. On the other hand, a business that is scaling up, or at scale, is any business that generates significant positive cash flows or earnings at a much faster rate than the overall economy.

Typically, these are businesses that operate with many people in more than one market and in multiple geographic regions. It's easy to think that a bigger business will make you happier, but that isn't always the case. There is nothing wrong with owning a profitable growth business. If it meets your lifestyle needs and fulfils you, then why not? But, whatever you do, don't chase the dream of owning a business at scale – a scale business – if that isn't what you actually want. The truth, your specific truth, as it relates to your why and your business, really matters.

Too many entrepreneurs are chasing the idea that 'bigger is better', and instead of finding happiness, they just end up miserable. They've lost their why – or they didn't know it in the first place. Building a big, fuck-off business is one thing. But doing that and holding onto your happiness and some semblance of balance at the same time is an entirely different challenge, and one you'll only conquer if what you're trying to achieve aligns with your truth.

Here's the thing: Too many entrepreneurs are chasing the kind of growth that will lead them to one day owning a business at scale, but they haven't paused to question if this is something that will make them happy. The CEO of a growth business and a CEO of a business at scale are very different. Many entrepreneurs want to scale, but they don't consider how it will fundamentally change their businesses and how the process of scaling will ask fundamentally different and bigger questions of the entrepreneur. Scaling may not be for you. You may not have the right character or possess the necessary skills to run a really big business.

There are two types of CEOs. The first is the market maker CEO. They are excellent at identifying a new category opportunity, building a great first product and creating the market for the thing that the business sells.

The second is the accumulation CEO. They maximise profits for the business and its shareholders and are able to manage the business at scale. It's rare to find a CEO who can do both, which means at some point the leadership of a scale up business needs to change. Take Travis Kalanick for example. Kalanick got Uber off the ground. As the business began to scale beyond all reasonable expectations, he was forced to resign as CEO of Uber amid reports of combative behaviour and an intellectual property lawsuit with self-driving rival Waymo. The company also faced allegations of a toxic work culture that led to widespread sexual harassment and gender discrimination. Uber at scale was a different kind of beast to the business that was founded as UberCab, an exciting new startup in 2009.

Unfortunately, most business owners think 'I have to scale' because of a media-driven and largely Silicon Valley narrative. A quick read of the front covers of business magazines will reveal titles like 'From Zero to a $100 Million in Two Years' (more on this later) and so what inevitably happens is a weird, peer-driven dynamic that prescribes that if an entrepreneur is going to be a success, then they have to build a scale business. Before you know it, what is motivating your growth as the founder is your ego instead of what you really want – and you don't even realise it. I know – I was a victim of this mentality for many years.

I'm going to circle back to Joey at this point. It was abundantly clear during our interview that he's always been clear on his why. I'm envious of his clarity. I haven't always known my own why, and it's led to decisions that haven't been best for me or my businesses.

The point is that you shouldn't be trying to grow your business unless you understand *why*. If you're just growing for the sake of growth, your passion and hunger for it will most likely fade (as it did with me, more than once), and then where will you be?

Consider the difference between these two entrepreneurs: If you're super-passionate about what it would take to build tens of thousands of restaurants that deliver top-quality food through a well-engineered supply chain, then growth drives you (again, we will meet an entrepreneur who is doing exactly this in Chapter 9). If, on the other hand, you take pride in having the best restaurant in your city, then focus on that – and forget about growth. Growth will not make you happy.

Scale should mean different things to different people. And above all else it should serve to make you happy, because what if you spend 20 years chasing scale and then, for whatever reason, it all falls away? What will you be left with? Worse, what if you achieve it, and realise it wasn't what you wanted in the first place? What have you sacrificed to reach that point? Remember, nothing worth having is easy, so you better know what it is that you're chasing.

What was your life about if you gave up spending time with your family, gave up your happiness and your smile, just for the sake of growth? Your *why* is everything, because it will help you to identify what motivates you, not only as an entrepreneur but as a human being. In my experience, most entrepreneurs are so busy chasing 'success' that they don't stop to think about what motivates them.

Joey was always crystal clear on this why. What motivated him to be successful was very simply to stick it to his physical ailments. He had what my good friend Brent Spilkin, a high-performance business coach, calls 'fuck you' motivation – which after making a difference to humanity is the next most powerful motivator that anyone can have.

HOW TO GET TO GRIPS WITH WHAT YOU WANT

Getting to grips with what you really want is not an easy thing to do. It's a paradox, because if you give yourself what you think you want, it's unlikely you'll give yourself what you need. The first step is to understand what the word 'scale' means to you, because despite dictionary and Wikipedia definitions, for every entrepreneur scale means something different. To get to the truth, you need to give your definition of scale context.

The first point to land is that there is a very Americanised view of scale, specifically within the venture capitalist and private equity space. Most notably, this is the narrative that comes out of Silicon Valley. Amazon, Uber, Airbnb, Netflix – these are all great examples of how we tend, traditionally, to view scale.

The media has a lot to do with playing up scale; especially in the Silicon Valley-dominated world of tech. Media outlets publish a seemingly endless series of headlines like: 'Postmates raises another $300M, reportedly valued at $1.2B'; 'Ola raises $50M at a $4.3B valuation from two Chinese funds'; or 'LimeBike raises $70 million as the bike-sharing battle rages on'. While none of these stories are untrue, they do paint a picture of scale and more broadly of entrepreneurship that isn't entirely accurate.

If startup-focused media was taken at face value, then any entrepreneur could start a business and six months later would sell that business for $100 million, move to the South of France to their multi-million dollar superyacht and live like a rock star doing Bolivian cocaine with a bunch of Russian supermodels – and all with other first-time founders who have 'made it' during the preceding six months.

Perception and reality are very different things. Many entrepreneurs who chase dreams and headlines of their own inevitably trip over reality and hit their head on the truth. That's okay. Failure is integral to the journey. Reality checks even more so. But if you want to be happy, build something meaningful and align your business with your values, it's important to realise that for every one of those 'zero to hero' headlines, there are hundreds of thousands of crushed entrepreneurial dreams littering sidewalks and coffee shops. Hundreds of thousands of stories that will never be covered in mainstream media because it's not cool to be the entrepreneur who couldn't scale and who loses their shirt in a failed startup.

This was one of the main reasons why I started my podcast. I'd experienced failed businesses more times than I cared to remember, and I wanted to paint the realities of entrepreneurship on the ground – not the glamour, but the cold, hard truth. I wanted to address the perceptions about scale that were being created by popularised media.

I love entrepreneurship. There's a reason I've built so many businesses, and why my podcast and business today are both focused on entrepreneurs. I can't imagine not being in this space. But like all things worth having, it's tough, and I've needed to come to terms with many truths to reach this point. I've needed to find my purpose and my why. I've needed to evaluate what success looks like for me, and where my balance between my family and my business lies. Most of all, I've needed to come to terms with what scale means to me.

Through my podcast, I've interviewed hundreds of successful entrepreneurs, billionaires on four different continents, venture capitalists, international best-selling authors and CEOs of some of the most exciting companies in the world, and the most fascinating thing I've taken away from these discussions is that while they all view scale differently, they also all do one thing consistently – they assign value to what the word 'scale' means in their own lives and businesses.

Think about it. If scaling a business doesn't hold any meaning for you, then it's unlikely that you will build a business at scale. You will always choose to pursue what you value, even if you don't realise it. But – and this is the crux of everything I've learned on this topic – if you do choose to pursue scale, then it's important that you don't fall into the trap of saying you want to build a business to scale, without really thinking about what that would mean for you personally and for your business.

When any entrepreneur is thinking about scale, it's important to understand that context matters. You see, for some people scale means growing from one shop to two shops, and that's fine. For another entrepreneur it might mean growing from one store to one thousand stores, and that's also fine. But before you can even start thinking or talking about scale, you need to understand what your relationship is with that number and that size. Because if you're going to try and produce a business that's a thousand times bigger than the one you currently have, when you're only comfortable with five times bigger, you're going to end up in a world of pain.

Enter Bob. Let's say that Bob is the founder of a tech startup called PyroTech based in Silicon Valley. Bob founded PyroTech because his 'why' was to build a software business that afforded him the time and the means to climb the seven summits of the world. Bob has bootstrapped the business and spent six months building a team and a minimum viable product (MVP), which his users love. The culture of the business is one of a very happy startup filled with anticipation of what lies in store for them and their shiny new tech product.

But competition is heating up and Bob decides that PyroTech needs to be the number one software product in the market, so now is the time to start scaling as his biggest competitor, DopeTech, has just raised $15 million in seed funding. Bob feels he has no choice but to hit up the VC network to remain competitive. After being turned down for investment fourteen times straight (this is not unusual) he finally lands a deal for a $10 million seed-round investment with Capricorn Inc, an exciting venture capital network that specialises in accelerating high-growth startups like PyroTech.

There are three general versions of what happens next. I'll begin with the most common scenario. The investors at Capricorn are hungry for growth. They want their pound of flesh and are looking for a 20x return on their investment over the next two years. It's game time for PyroTech. At the insistence of Capricorn, Bob has to make some structural changes within the company to enable the expected growth and investment returns. A new executive team is established comprising of a hot-shot Sales Director, Chief Marketing Officer (CMO), Chief Operations Officer (COO), Chief Data Officer (CDO) and Talent Manager. Scalable operational systems are installed, along with a new set of business processes and a way of working that supports the desired scale. Naturally, Bob's original team don't like these changes, and they complain to Bob about the direction in which PyroTech is heading. Bob tells them not to worry and that things will improve.

Meanwhile, Capricorn request bi-weekly meetings with Bob and the rest of the executive team to review PyroTech's sales performance and financial projections. Cash burn and an exponential growth strategy becomes a primary focus for the business and Capricorn decides that it's time for the business to go after a bigger but more competitive market to help achieve this desired growth. Bob starts to realise that his vision for PyroTech is shifting to that of his investors and the new executive team and as a result the culture of PyroTech is also slowly, but surely, changing. A few members of his original founding team leave despite Bob's objections and attempts to get them to stay.

Six months later, sales begin to slow due to stiffer competition present in the new market and Capricorn puts Bob under more and more pressure to hit sales targets. Despite his best efforts, PyroTech sales remain stagnant and unfortunately for Bob, Capricorn decides that he is no longer the right CEO to be leading the company. Bob is told that he's a great founder but not the right CEO to lead and enable their high-growth strategy. Bob is ousted as CEO of PyroTech and asked to be a non-executive Chairman, while a new CEO is installed. Bob is left dejected about the entire experience and regrets not bootstrapping the business for another year or two – had he done that he would have been able to remain in control of PyroTech.

In the second version of the story, Bob remains CEO and the business does well. It achieves the scale Capricorn was looking for and sales are great, rising steadily year-on-year. However, most of the founding team has left, the business does not resemble the startup Bob created in the first place and its culture is unrecognisable. Bob has also not climbed a single summit since he launched the business, which was one of his original goals.

This kind of story (version one and two) is not uncommon in the world of high-growth tech startups, with the average founder not understanding the consequences of scaling with venture capital. If only Bob had remembered *why* he started PyroTech in the first place: to afford himself the financial means and the time required to climb the seven summits of the world. He didn't need to be the number one software product in the market; he just needed it to be the favourite software product for a certain amount of loyal users. He needed a *lifestyle* business. Not a scale business. To do that, PyroTech could have been the number two or number three software product in the market. Unfortunately for Bob, the Silicon Valley narrative was the only winner at the end of the day.

I haven't forgotten the third version of this story, the version where once Bob launches his business, he realises that his main driving force *is* to become the number one software product in the world. He chases venture capital to achieve this goal and is willing to give up any, and all, other dreams for this new vision. He wants to be a scale business and will do everything necessary to achieve it.

If this is your goal, then chase it. Don't let anyone tell you otherwise. But before you buy into the scale narrative just for the sake of it, understand that scale isn't for everyone. I know many successful and, more importantly, happy entrepreneurs who don't own a scale business: bloggers, freelancers, restaurant owners, salon owners, boutique consulting firms, creative agencies, the list goes on. Many of these entrepreneurs do not want to scale simply because their business suits their lifestyle needs and personal ambitions.

At the end of the day, there are many different versions of scale – and they're all personal. When it comes to your personal code as an entrepreneur, your 'why' is arguably the most important principle. So, let's try and get clear on that right now.

TO SCALE OR NOT TO SCALE?

Questions govern our lives more than we care to admit. Indira Gandhi said it best: 'The power to question is the basis of all human progress.' There can be no better example to illustrate the direct relationship between questions and human progress than during the Space Race between Russia and the United States.

In 1962, John F. Kennedy gave his famous 'we choose to go to the moon' speech and just 2 503 days later Neil Armstrong and pilot Buzz Aldrin stepped onto the moon. It was indeed a small step for man, but a giant leap for mankind. The entire world celebrated the moon landing. We marvelled at a new dawn of human achievement and the possibilities that lay before us. Yet, despite all the innovation that had occurred as a result of the Space Race, there was plenty more waiting in the wings. One of those innovations was wheeled luggage. That's right, we put a man on the moon 13 years before we put wheels on luggage. Why? Because the best minds in the world were focused on putting a man on the moon, not making normal travel a bit easier.

This same principle is true for you, because as an entrepreneur on any given day, you can create any number of possible futures for your business and for yourself. And so, the question becomes how do you create the future you truly desire? Well, the simple way is to ask better questions, because if you don't ask the right questions you'll never get the right answers. You will always be acting on less-than-okay information. And with less-than-okay information you will inevitably make less-than-okay decisions. And decisions are your ultimate power. Whether you choose to scale or not, your decisions today will always predict the outcomes of tomorrow.

So, what kind of questions should you be asking? Start by asking yourself: What do I want? Do you want to make the human race a multi-planetary species and colonise Mars like Elon Musk? Do you want to prove to your dad that you can build a bigger business than he ever could? Do you want to build a bigger business than your ex-wife's new partner? Do you want to live a simple life in relative isolation, made possible by an online information product business that makes $50 000 a month?

Next, ask yourself why? For example, if you want to build a billion-dollar business, then ask yourself why? It may be because you want people to admire your achievements or maybe your risk radar is broken and you'll do anything just to see if you can pull it off. At its essence, it's about understanding what motivates you as a human being. The world's leading expert on the human psyche, Tony Robbins, suggests that there are six needs that drive us as humans. These are broken down by the four needs of the personality and the two needs of the soul.

The needs of the personality:

- Certainty – the desire to know what is going to happen.
- Uncertainty – the desire and appetite for risk.
- Love – the desire to connect with people.

- Significance – the desire to be seen and admired by others.

The needs of the soul:

- Growth – the desire to grow and improve.
- Contribution – the desire to give back.

Most of us are motivated by one or two of these needs more than the others. If you were to select two of these six, what would they be? How can you see these needs being expressed in your behaviours and, importantly, in the things that you want for yourself and for your business?

The thing about your motivations and the goals you set for yourself is that they *will* change over time. When I was in my twenties, when someone asked me what I wanted out of life, my need for significance would kick in and I would say, 'I want to be the owner of a billion-dollar business.' But when I'm asked that question today, the answer is all about contribution. Most entrepreneurs go through this same transformation. My good friend Rich Mulholland, who is one of South Africa's (if not the world's) best speakers, says it best: 'When I was 20, I wanted to be a billionaire. When I was 30, I realised that I probably would never be one, and at the age of 40 I stopped giving a fuck.' He's busy building a great new startup that he plans to scale around the world, but his *why* has changed.

What I have observed about the motivations of the entrepreneurs who have built businesses to scale, is that they are very rarely – if ever – motivated by material things. Since the very first interview I conducted on my podcast, my last question to every guest has been this: 'Why do you do what you do? What gets you out of bed in the morning?' You may be surprised to learn that I've never received an answer that had anything to do with wanting to be successful, or about chasing a number in a bank account.

In fact, the large majority are motivated by spiritual needs, a deep desire for personal growth and a need to contribute to humanity and the world around them. In all cases, there is a great deal of meaning attached to their actions. Joey Evans overcame the almost impossible challenge of his paralysis and finished the Dakar Rally as a result. True Inner Game has, at its core, unequivocal meaning. This feeds into purpose, motivation and perseverance.

Back to growth versus scale businesses. The biggest difference I've encountered between an entrepreneur who chooses to build a growth business versus one who chooses to pursue a scale business comes down to one thing – hunger.

'Scalepreneurs' or entrepreneurs who do build a business to scale, remain hungry despite their successes. It's never about the money. Instead, their motivations are firmly placed in the areas of uncertainty, growth and contribution and they have an insatiable fascination and curiosity to see how big something can become. Their love for the game of business is tireless and they rarely, if ever, regard themselves as successful. If this sounds like you, then you are probably chasing a scale business and I would also bet that you are not reading these words by chance.

A QUESTION OF PURPOSE

The idea of purpose was gifted to me by my father when I was 10 years old. It was 6 am one Sunday morning in the sleepy suburb of Table View in Cape Town. I was awake, but my parents were still sleeping. I had a friend, Mark, who lived a few blocks down the road, so I headed out on my bicycle to wake him up for some playtime before Sunday School. A short while later I was knocking on Mark's front door, he opened up and all was well. Until we got bored.

In 1989, Table View was a small suburb surrounded by wild bush, but it was expanding rapidly and there were a lot of property and housing developments going up. Just across from Mark's house was a series of houses that had recently been plastered with fresh cement. Bored stiff, we thought it would be a great idea to run our fingers through the walls of the wet cement of these new houses and so we did. Any wet wall we could find became a target. In all the fun I forgot about the one thing I was forbidden to miss – Sunday School.

The next thing I know I heard my dad's voice from behind me: 'Matthew! What the fuck are you doing? You naughty little shit! Get your ass home immediately; we'll have to talk about this when we get back as your mother and I are late for church.'

By 'talk', what he actually meant was that I was going to get a beat down. In a panic and convinced my life was about to end, I raced back home. As soon as I arrived, I started frantically cleaning the house, making beds, tidying up the kitchen – things I would ordinarily never do, but, hey, when you're convinced you're going to take the beat down of all beat downs, you do whatever you must to dodge the consequences. After what felt like several days, my parents arrived home and of course my old man sends me to my room for 'our talk'. Sitting on the end of my bed, I felt the adrenaline pumping through my veins.

In walks my dad. I prepared inwardly for my impending death. But, instead, he sat down next to me and out came the following words: 'You know Matt, I need to speak to you about something. At the end of your life, God is going to ask you what the purpose of your life was and you'd better have a good answer. Also, I don't want you seeing that Mark kid anymore. He's a bad influence on you.'

There was no beat down. Talk about a get out of jail free card. I said: 'Sure Dad, absolutely. I'll *find* my purpose one day for sure.' Counting my lucky stars, I'm not sure I meant it in that moment, but the idea of finding my purpose had been seeded and has caused me sleepless nights ever since.

During my early entrepreneurial endeavours, I didn't have a real purpose. I just wanted to make something of myself. Whenever I tried to ask myself questions like, 'what is the purpose of my life?' I'd just end up freaking out. No clear ideas magically presented themselves. And so, for years I meandered along, wondering when I would suddenly find my purpose and finally become the hero in my own story.

You know that guy who is an absolute savage in business, and unstoppable in the face of any and all adversity – all thanks to having a clear purpose? That's who I wanted to be. It took me many years to work out that when it comes to purpose, you'll never just find it. You need to create it, and that takes focus and time.

I've found two approaches that work well when it comes to creating purpose. The first is to decide on a problem the world has and then go out there and solve it. A great example of this is Elon Musk and SpaceX. Elon's overriding belief is that the human race will have a serious problem on its hands should an extinction-level event occur on Earth. He, therefore, created SpaceX, a privatised space exploration company that is attempting to make the human race a multi-planetary species. The second approach, and one of the most compelling ways I have found to explore the question of purpose deeply and authentically, is to talk about your own death. So, let's talk about death.

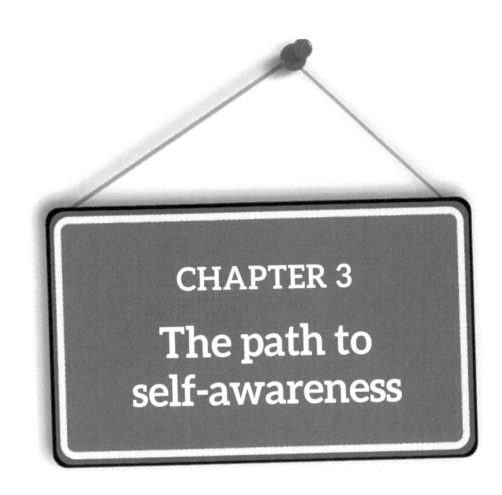

CHAPTER 3

The path to
self-awareness

Player:	**Robin Wheeler,** author of *Death is the Ultimate Orgasm*
Episode:	MBS118
Principle:	*I will not live in regret*

In the end, we only regret the chances we didn't take.

– ANONYMOUS

*T*here are many conversations that you can have with yourself about why you do what you do, but the most revealing will be a conversation that involves your death. Death is a subject that we rarely, if ever, talk about around the dinner table. In fact, we don't like talking about it period, and for good reason. The certainty of death is absolute, and it scares the hell out of us.

We also don't really know what happens to us when we die and that presents a real problem, because it's easy to fall into a trap of thinking that what we fear is the unknown. In fact, what we're really afraid of is the known coming to an end.

Here's the thing though, there's a lot of power to be found in facing up to the idea of death, because it forces you to have an honest and authentic conversation with yourself about *why* you do what you do and what gets you out of bed in the morning. Once you know that, everything, from your life to your business to your family, starts falling into place. You just have to be willing to face it.

Robin Wheeler is the author of the book *Death is the Ultimate Orgasm*. His message is simple: be yourself for a living. He uses ancient spirituality and the current world of music, business and entrepreneurship and turns it into a modern vernacular that helps people live on a higher level of consciousness for a new age.

During my interview with Robin, he summed up death for entrepreneurs. 'Death and life are inseparable. The moment you are conceived, your death is immediately built into that. If you want to be realistic about your purpose in life, you have to embrace the fact that you are going to die.

Otherwise you're living in delusion, and if you're living in delusion you can't live properly. So, if you want to truly live, you need to embrace death.'

Robin runs retreats all around the world. One of these retreats is in Rishikesh in India. Retreat-goers visit cemeteries to sit and meditate among the graves. 'To the average westerner this sounds hectic, but we do this to wake people up. If you can't face the reality that you will die then you are not living in reality. Death is integral to life because we are living and dying all the time. To embrace this fact is to live in a fully conscious way by integrating all areas of your life.'

There are many similarities between death and business. Businesses are created and born every day. We nurture the business for years and then one day it dies. When this happens, the grief is personal, and in the process we're reborn as entrepreneurs. As it is in life, so, too, in business: death is inevitable. Face this truth and you can truly start living within your business, instead of being held back by fear.

A simple example of how an entrepreneur can become more self-aware is cash flow. 'Entrepreneurs have to survive their worst fears and one of those fears is running out of money. Imagine that you have staff to pay but you don't have enough cash. You scramble for days trying to make ends meet and the night before all those debit orders are going to go through you feel like your world is about to end. But then in the morning, you open one eye and you realise that while you might not have any money, your world has not ended. You're not dead. In fact, you're still very much alive. That's all you've got. You're not dead. And then you realise that, okay, I was living with a certain sense of myself and now I've awakened to a deeper sense of self that actually bridges those gaps, and you become aware of a self who can survive those challenges, and that resilience is what becomes the seasoned entrepreneur. And that's the one who ultimately succeeds: The one who knows who he or she is. So, death is essential in an entrepreneur's life,' Robin told me.

Becoming self-aware as an entrepreneur is a conscious and life-long endeavour. It's also an essential ingredient to leading a successful and happy life, because self-awareness precedes choice and choice precedes results. You also have to be consciously open to your death in order to develop an insatiable curiosity; a desire to seek the truth about who you are as a human being first and as an entrepreneur second.

Enter Aristotle. Aristotle lived between 384 BC and 322 BC and was an ancient Greek philosopher and scientist born in the city of Stagira, Chalkidiki, Greece. Along with Plato, he is considered to be the 'Father of Western Philosophy', which means he's accredited with being one very smart dude who was incredibly curious about pretty much everything.

In fact, he was so intelligent and curious that society sentenced him to death. Says Robin, 'Society told him to either leave or drink poison. He chose to drink the poison because, in his words, he had truly lived. A short while after drinking the poison, he couldn't feel his feet, to which he said "I can't feel my feet, but I am still here, so I am not my feet." When his legs went numb, he said, "I may not feel my legs, but I am still here so who is left?" To reach a higher level of awareness requires us to embrace death in a curious, courageous and open manner, so that ultimately we can discover a greater sense of the truth about who we are, what makes us tick and the change we want to make in the world as entrepreneurs.'

EMBRACING DEATH REVEALS PURPOSE

Dr Adriana Marais is a physicist, innovator and aspiring extra-terrestrial. Since childhood, she has dreamed of living on another planet and is currently one of the one hundred Mars One Project astronaut candidates in the running to move to the red planet in the next decade. Mars One plans to be the first company to colonise Mars.

The humans who go on this mission are not going to come back to Earth. They will die on Mars. They are not only choosing to die on a different planet, but to leave everyone and everything they know and love to get onto a spaceship that may or may not reach its destination. And if it does reach Mars, that's it, they're stuck there for life. There's no going back.

Adriana fascinates me. I asked her why she was doing this and she said: 'The reason I want to go to Mars is simple: I have to go. The allure of the unknown is far more powerful than the comfort of the known.' What she's doing terrifies me, but when you meet her, one thing is very clear: she knows exactly what she wants. Death doesn't scare her – not living the life she wants scares her. By accepting the inevitability of death, she's able to chase this incredible, crazy, life-changing dream.

I'm not saying we should all have a dream as extreme as Adriana's, but we do need to start thinking about our purpose – what holds meaning for you? You only get this one life to live, so what do you want it to mean when it ends?

If you want to get to a deeper sense of your purpose then at some point you need to have a 'come to Jesus' conversation with yourself and the best way to do that is to think about your death. It will force you to ask and, more importantly, answer the big questions about your life. Who am I? What legacy do I want to leave behind? What is the purpose of my life? What do I *really* need? *Why* do I do what I do?

At some point, I will reach the moment of my death. When that happens, there will be two questions that will reign supreme. The first is, 'who did I become?' For me at least, being an entrepreneur is less about acquiring more; it's about becoming more.

Stop for a moment and imagine that this is the day of your funeral. Two of your friends are chatting and sharing anecdotes. And then one raises the topic of who you became in life. What are they saying to each other? How are they describing your growth and journey? Really imagine hearing the actual words. Would you want them to say that?

Imagine they're talking about what an inspiring entre-preneur you were, how you changed the world, leaving it a better place. Now imagine they're talking about the really big business you built, becoming a billionaire, except you didn't do much with your wealth or influence. How do these two separate narratives make you feel?

The second question is about who you have helped. Every incredibly successful entrepreneur and human being I've interviewed has a deep need to contribute to humanity and the world around them. So, on the day of your funeral, are people only going to talk about how you helped yourself, or are they going to talk about the millions of people you mentored and helped through your business endeavours?

Many entrepreneurs get so caught up in the pursuit of material things and the running of the business itself that they don't stop to think about how they can make a positive difference to those around them at the same time. Don't get me wrong. I'm certainly guilty of this too. But I've come to realise that it's not the best way to build or run a business – and it's certainly not the best way to live life. It's small thinking for even smaller rewards.

Marc Benioff, the founder and CEO of Salesforce, (and whose net worth is currently north of $6 billion) is actively asking entrepreneurs around the world to pledge 1% of their most important resources (product, time and equity) to support the integration of this philosophy into their businesses from an early stage. Marc has built a business to scale. Salesforce is an international market leader. But he understands the value of contribution as an entrepreneur and that you don't need to be running a non-profit social enterprise to do it. You can make money and a difference at the same time.

The challenge with contribution, of course, is that your ego is always messing with your shit. Your ego will fuck with your reality, decision making and, most certainly, with your idea of contribution. Your ego will convince you that contribution should not be the goal; instead, it will drive you to accumulating things that involve status, power and success. But, underneath that veil is the need for something authentic and the experience of living a life filled with meaning and purpose. But you need to lift the veil and let your true self out.

It's only in the absence of being fully alive that we look for substitutes in material things. When we acquire them, we then look to get more and more of the same, until a wealth of possessions become a monument to an unfulfilled life. Don't get me wrong. I like living a comfortable life, and entrepreneurship can support that – a nice house, private school for my kids and hobbies I enjoy. But without purpose, it can be pretty empty, particularly when you're working 20-hour days and have forgotten your why.

Getting over ego is never an easy thing to do – and entrepreneurs tend to have a lot of ego. As a result, we deal with the endless and inevitable consequence of ambition in life and in business.

There's an argument to be made that ego exists to serve our best interests, but it can also quickly undermine the same dreams it's supposed to be helping us achieve. The irony is that we are offered very little help with this dilemma in life, and even less so in the context of business and entrepreneurship.

There's no manual for entrepreneurs that accurately describes the inner workings of our ego and its influence on our choices. There's certainly nothing that describes how to deal with our ego-driven selves in a simple, effective and repeatable manner. We need our egos to navigate the business world, to guide our instincts and to drive our personal ambitions. But we also need to recognise that, in the context of ego and scale, we all suffer from a split-personality disorder in which our present self wants a specific thing (that billion-dollar business), but our future or past self wants a different thing (a life filled with meaning and purpose). And this is the business of 'Egonomics', so prevalent in the entrepreneurial world.

Author Gaurav Madan defines 'Egonomics' as a composite of two terms – 'Ego' and 'omics'. In his view, Ego is our self-awareness, the part of the mind that mediates between the conscious and the unconscious and is responsible for reality testing, and also a sense of personal identity. However, the suffix –omics derives its meaning from biology. In other words, a study in the totality of an entity, which in this case is the Self. He suggests 'Egonomics' is a process of developing holistic awareness of 'awareness' itself.

At the core of Egonomics is the idea that within every entrepreneur exists two selves: The past or future self and the present self, constantly at odds, leading to a sort of cognitive dissonance between the two. Both selves exist within us and are equally valid, but aren't always active at the same time. It's a natural and ongoing conflict between immediate desire and long-term desires, the longing to build a big business versus the longing for meaning.

Simply put, because of our egos, on any given day we can behave like two different people. For example, one who wants clean lungs and a long, healthy life and the other who can't wait to light up that first cigarette over a hot cup of coffee in the morning. Or how about the person who wants a fit and lean body and the same person who can't stop eating chocolates or sweets? In the context of entrepreneurship, it's the aspiring entrepreneur who wants to build a business, but then doesn't put in the hard work every single day and who isn't prepared to make the necessary sacrifices, both big and small, to get there. Alternatively, it's the scale-based entrepreneur who would really be happier with a lifestyle business that supports playing golf three times a week. It all comes down to figuring out what we really want – and then going for it with everything we have.

There are many shapes and forms of Egonomics – it comes down to our own level of self-awareness. When it comes to Inner Game, I believe the happiest and most successful entrepreneurs (in life, not turnover size) have found a way to balance 'ego' and 'omics'.

When I started podcasting, my purpose was simple: To help entrepreneurs succeed through information sharing at scale. Like Joey Evans, I didn't find my purpose, I created it. If you are in need of a life filled with purpose, Robin says that thinking about your death is the bottom line of all things. 'Death is the greatest advisor you can have. Even Steve Jobs said that "death is very likely the single best invention of life". You have to go on an inward journey of death, because you'll never survive the stress of entrepreneurship and self-actualisation without that depth. Be yourself for a living. Business just follows on from that.'

Self-discovery is at the centre of everything we do. Today, when I consider the first podcast I ever did, I can see clearly the extraordinary journey of transformation I've been on, and everything I've learned over the past four years. I'm also aware that my motivations came from a place of contribution, which is what makes this endeavour so different from many that came before it.

Because of this, I have built the most amazing network around the world, signed multiple book deals, built a business that has quadrupled in size in only six months, was voted as the Best Tech Startup in Africa in 2019 and expanded into the US, with a second office in Austin, Texas.

Looking back, I sincerely doubt that any of this would have been possible if I hadn't learned how to be clear on my own 'why' and what my true motivations are as an entrepreneur. Without these fundamental elements of my own code in place, I would never have been able to start living my life to its fullest potential. The antithesis of a life of regret is having a code and a set of principles to live by. We need that roadmap.

DEATH AND REGRET

Rich Mulholland is the founder of Cultivation, a holding company for a number of innovative businesses, one of which was his first company, Missing Link. Two decades after he launched it, Missing Link is one of the world's leading presentation companies. It was while he was wrestling with the idea of whether or not he should step away from Missing Link to pursue a new business idea that he wrote a talk entitled *How Not to Live With Regret*.

He was in the middle of a life-changing decision himself, but the talk was triggered by an experience he'd had with his great aunt. Two days before she died, Rich walked into her room and she was crying. Here's the backstory: when she was 20, she fell in love with a man who wasn't Catholic. When her parents found out they forbade her from ever seeing him again. Even though he had proposed, she did what they said, and she never spoke to him again. More than 66 years later, on her deathbed, she was crying because she was wondering what her life would have been like if she'd married Leslie John Moore. Her dying days were spent regretting a decision she herself hadn't made.

This story really makes me appreciate how Robin views death. We need to think about our final days. Thinking about death holds a mirror up to our lives today, and the decisions we are making in the here and now.

Entrepreneurship must be worth something more than just the accumulation of material things. The irony of regret is that it isn't based on what you achieve, but rather on what you didn't do. For instance, you'll never regret not building a big business if you gave it your best shot. But you will regret not trying if that's what you'd love to achieve.

Rich's talk had over 17 million views on Goalcast's Facebook page at the time this book went to print. Not living with regret seems to be something we are all very interested in achieving, and yet so few of us look ahead enough to ensure we're making the right decisions today to be truly happy tomorrow.

CHAPTER 4

Harness your fears

Player:	**Allon Raiz**, CEO Raizcorp
Episode:	MBS025, MBS105 and MBS143
Principle:	*I will not be fearless. I will be fear*-less

Named must your fear be
before banish it you can.

- YODA

*A*llon Raiz is the founder of Raizcorp, a business prosperator that supports the growth of entrepreneurs. Raizcorp currently looks after about 500 businesses across South Africa, Angola, Zimbabwe and Tanzania, and about 12 000 businesses have graduated from Raizcorp's programmes over the past two decades.

Allon launched his first business when he was 23. It was called the New York Sausage Factory and it was in Pinetown, near Durban. It was an abysmal failure. The worst thing about it all was that an accountant had done the numbers and he told Allon it would be a failure, but he went ahead and did it anyway because he was young, arrogant and thought he knew better. He tried to make the business work. He put everything he had into it; he had a mentor and an investor whom he regularly asked for advice – and it still failed. When you have all the ingredients and a business still fails, there's only one place left to look: the entrepreneur. Allon needed to recognise that he, alone, was responsible for the failure of his business – he couldn't blame anyone or anything else.

He finally plucked up the courage to go and see his investor to tell him that if it took him the rest of his life, he would pay him back. The investor's response was unexpected. He looked at Allon and asked, 'Did I back you, or did I back the business?' Allon replied that he had backed him. 'Well, right now,' he replied, 'the business has failed. But if you walk out that door, it will be you who has failed. What did you do wrong and what will you do differently the next time?'

The investor knew that what he needed was people – a team – not money. And so, in his next business, his investor backed him with people instead of money. But Allon learned a valuable lesson about fear that day. 'If something fails, I'll be depressed for a while, but I'll get back up and try again,' he told me. 'That's who I am. I know that as long as I get back up again, *I* won't fail.'

The first step to overcoming the fear factor is recognising you have it – everyone does; we're all human. But some people are able to go out, pursue their dreams and take risks regardless of that fear, and others aren't.

There's a concept in entrepreneurship called re-entry rate, which is basically the number of times an entrepreneur comes back after failure. In the US, it's 3.6 times – that's the average. In South Africa it's 1.1 times. Most entrepreneurs in this country fail once and never come back. We try, we fail, and we go and get a job.

Allon's relationship with fear and failure is different. Sure, we make mistakes. Yes, we fail. But there are so many lessons to learn when that happens and you can come back and take those lessons and do something great. But you have to be willing to try. Allon lives in fear that his business will fail every day. But he will not live in fear that *he* will fail. And to him there's a huge difference.

HOW TO BECOME FEAR-*LESS*

Consider the relationship between fear and Inner Game. Some of us are born with stronger Inner Game than others, but like any muscle it can be worked and built up. I'll be covering this more in different contexts later, but for now, a key factor in real, strong and, above-all, enduring Inner Game is the ability to look fear in the face, admit it's there – and then be courageous anyway. This doesn't mean be stupid, bet your kids' college fund on a risky business bet, or allow your big, brass balls to rule you in the face of all evidence telling you you're pursuing a bad idea.

But it does mean that entrepreneurship is scary as hell and most of the fears that you're facing daily are not only baseless, but can be controlled.

Everyone's fears are different. You can't lump them all into one basket. They're deeply personal. If you want to build your Inner Game, you need to figure out what it is you're scared of, and then how you're going to conquer those fears.

It's easy to think that entrepreneurs like Elon Musk or Richard Branson are fearless, but this isn't the case. Like you and me, they're human. But there is a reason why entrepreneurs like Zuckerberg, Bezos, Jobs, Musk and Branson have dominated their markets. They don't operate in the absence of fear, but they are fear-*less*. In a nutshell, they're able to act despite their fear. Colonise Mars? Sure. Launch Virgin Galactic, a space flight company? Why not?

This same truth has shone through in many of my interviews of the highly successful. The lesson is that your ability to take on greater challenges in business is directly proportional to your ability to be fear-*less*. This doesn't mean we have no fears – all entrepreneurs have fears; some more than others. In many instances we let our fears stifle our courage and our capacity to push through the challenges that lie in front of us. We need to find a way to fear *less* than we do right now.

There is an old eastern fable about a traveller who began a long journey across a treacherous mountain range. While on a steep mountain pass, the sun began to set and nightfall closed in. During the night, the traveller lost his way under cloud cover and was forced to stop in complete darkness. Not being able to see anything, he spent the night gripped by fear that he would roll over in his sleep and fall off the cliff to his certain death. He didn't sleep a wink. When morning broke, he opened his eyes to discover that he was on a giant ledge at the top of a mountain and that no threat had existed at all. Fear is a tricky thing. It's usually not rational, and yet it grabs hold of us with such strength that no amount of logic can shake it.

On an evolutionary level, fear has a very important purpose: it helps us to avoid physical harm and death. It's an undeniably significant survival tool. But that's it. That's the thing and the whole of the thing. It serves no other role. And yet so many of us end up ruled by irrational fears.

As entrepreneurs, we end up using fear as a tool to protect our own egos, because, like Allon did during the failure of his first business, we think that failure in business is the same as failing personally. Inevitably, we play small so that we can protect ourselves from the threat of our own greatness.

Over the years, I have discovered that you get two types of entrepreneurs: those who let their fears define them, and those who use their fears to push them forward. The latter are those who inevitably go on to either build scale businesses or are truly able to find their purpose and will chase it, no matter what obstacles they encounter. The former never will.

The secret to living in a fear-*less* way is to describe the nightmare – the absolute worst-case scenario. What would you lose? What would it cost you? Approach your fears with curiosity while simultaneously observing your reaction. When you're scared of doing something, it's because you're thinking of all the things that could go wrong, instead of just jumping into it and realising that it's okay. What if you could take all of that shit, say fuck it, and do it anyway?

Tim Ferriss talks about a quote that changed his life by Seneca the Younger, a famous Stoic writer: 'We suffer more often in imagination than in reality.' Ferriss took a deep dive into Seneca the Younger's letters because of this idea, and from there he discovered the practice of visualising worst-case scenarios. The purpose is straightforward: Imagine in detail the fear that is preventing you from taking action. Really live it. Write it down. Ferriss uses an exercise that he calls 'fear-setting'. It consists of three pages.

Page one is his 'What if I ...' page. This is where you capture the action that is causing the fear. He splits the page into three columns. Column one is where he defines the fear and lists all the worst things he can imagine happening if he takes the step that is causing him anxiety. The next column is his 'prevent' column, which is where he tackles each point in the first column – how can he prevent them from happening, or at least decrease their likelihood. The third column is 'repair'. If the worst case does happen anyway, what steps can be taken to repair the damage, even just a little bit?

The second page takes a different angle: What are the benefits of at least attempting the step, particularly if you are able to achieve even partial success? So far, Ferriss is playing up his fears and only taking a conservative look at the upside of actually taking the step.

Page three is the most important page. Here, Ferriss lists the 'Cost of Inaction' – and this is where most entrepreneurs really lose out because of fear paralysis. There is always a cost to not taking that leap, and those costs add up.

'Humans are very good at considering what might go wrong if we try something new. What we don't often consider is the atrocious cost of the status quo – not changing anything,' says Ferriss.

On this page, ask yourself what will happen if you avoid this action or decision, or actions and decisions like it. What will your life or business look like in six or even 12 months? Will you be achieving your goals? Will you be building the business you're hoping for? We end up so wrapped up in our own fears that we forget just how high the cost of inaction can be.

This exercise can be scary as hell – the realities of fear paralysis can be far more terrifying than the fear that's holding you back, which is the whole point of it in the first place.

Since he started fear-setting, Ferriss says that he can trace all of his biggest wins and all of his biggest disasters *averted*, to this exercise. This doesn't mean that some fears aren't well-founded, but it is a way to address them without allowing them to completely hold you back. Inaction is always worse than action – even the wrong action. Don't end up living in regret because of choices you *didn't* make.

Allon also points out that we don't need to be alone in this journey. Mentorship and partnerships can play a key role. When I first interviewed Allon in my 25th episode, he gave a great piece of advice to entrepreneurs for overcoming their fears: 'Find someone whose perspective you trust and ask them to hold a mirror up to your fears. Ask them whether you're thinking about things rationally. Basically, find someone who you can lock arms with, and who will jump off the bridge with you.'

Allon is a scale-up entrepreneur. It's not about the money – he just wants to see how big he can build his business. He's also helping thousands of entrepreneurs, which gives what he's doing real meaning and purpose. But he had to decide to jump. He had to face his failures and his fears and get back up. No matter what your goal is, you have to make those decisions, too. *You* have to decide to jump. Nobody can do this for you. You have to decide – and I mean *really* decide – what you want, so that you can figure out what fears are holding you back. It's okay to fail – as we've seen, it comes with the territory. But at least you won't regret not having tried.

The crazy thing about fear is that it's not real. It's a projection of the future that you are bringing into the now. Ninety per cent of the things that I have feared, in both business and personally as an entrepreneur, have never happened. I mean literally never happened. Not even close.

When I look back at all the time I spent wrapped up in fear over things that were beyond my control, I can't help but wonder what I could have done if I used that time to better direct my energies towards more positive outcomes.

In almost every case, the only thing to fear is fear itself. If you choose to live in fear (and it is a conscious choice) then you will be miserable. If you don't break through that pattern, then you must learn to be happy in your misery. The alternative is to *choose* to be fear-*less*. To quote the great Nelson Mandela: 'I learned that courage was not the absence of fear, but the triumph over it. The brave man is not he who is afraid but he who conquers that fear.'

Embrace fear, face it, and you can teach yourself to jump. To repeat what I said at the beginning of this chapter: becoming fear-*less* is like any other muscle – it needs to be worked. Thinking vaguely about our fears paralyses us. The problem is that we are all very good at embracing the negative narrative in our heads (in fact we are genetically hardwired to default to the negative) and that keeps us stuck in the same place. Let's rather work on our Inner Game, develop a set of principles to live by, look for solutions instead – and then nurture the perseverance to see them through.

CHAPTER 5

The power of
perseverance

Player:	**Richard Wright**
Episode:	MBS142
Principle:	*I will persevere*

Great works are performed not
by strength but by perseverance.

– *SAMUEL JOHNSON*

*P*erseverance is failing 19 times and succeeding on the twentieth. Two famous Thomas Edison quotes sum it up nicely: 'I have not failed. I've just found 10 000 ways that won't work.' And of course, 'Many of life's failures are people who did not realise how close they were to success when they gave up.'

Both sum up the importance of perseverance. In entrepreneurial circles, we often talk about the ten-year overnight success. What this is referring to is businesses that are 'suddenly' successful, in the media – indeed, everywhere you look – and the impression is that this success was achieved overnight, when in fact the founders have been patiently plugging away for years, not letting their failures hold them back.

We don't always hear these back stories and the reality is that many businesses and careers don't make it. But those who persevere often do – eventually.

What I've learned through the many incredible people that I've interviewed however, is that challenges come in many different shapes and sizes. We don't all have the same burden to bear. But we can learn from each other, support each other, and take inspiration from how others have persevered, often against the most impossible odds. Some of the stories that have been shared with me make what I've gone through pale in comparison. It's an important – and humbling – lesson.

When someone tells you that you're going to die – that you have six months left to live, and you'll never see another Christmas – it's almost a gift. That's what Richard

Wright told me when I interviewed him for the show. And he was speaking from experience.

Richard is the 118th human to survive a rare, but extremely aggressive form of cancer, of the pituitary gland. He's currently got cancer for the third time, and he continues to fight. He's also a father, has finished 11 Ironmans and believes that we shouldn't need to be told we're about to die to live our most authentic lives.

YOU CAN'T FINISH WHAT YOU DON'T START

In late 2015, Richard was training for the Ironman when he began to realise that something was seriously wrong. He'd been living with a tumour on his pituitary gland for 12 years, and with medication everything had been under control. The amount of time it was taking him to recover from training, however, was painting a different picture, and so he went for an MRI scan.

'The MRI didn't look good, but it also wasn't conclusive,' he told me. 'Bloods also can't tell if you have a cancerous tumour. You need a lumbar puncture so that your spinal fluid can be tested, which I wasn't prepared to do just before my race.'

Richard's doctor wasn't happy with his decision, but he was comfortable with his own choice. 'Not racing wasn't an option for me. I told my doctor I was good at managing my body, and that if I couldn't finish, so be it. Not finishing was better than not starting. A DNS was far, far worse than a DNF for me, because I'd be giving up before I'd even begun.'

Richard finished that race through pure grit and determination. In his own words, his mind overrode his body. We're talking about a 3,8 kilometre sea swim, 180 kilometres on a bicycle and a 42 kilometre marathon. But – and this is what Richard really highlights, and what got him through that race in 2015 – you have 17 hours to do it in.

'In my mind, every single person is capable of finishing the Ironman if you can walk, swim and ride a bike. The minute you think *you can't* versus *you can* though, you're 100% correct.'

And so, Richard didn't let his brain limit him, focusing on each next small goal in the race. He had 17 hours to do this in. He just needed to finish. And with that mindset, he found the will to persevere and finish the Ironman. Richard firmly believes that the Ironman is like most things in life; if you don't start, the battle is over before it even begins.

Five days later, a lumbar puncture revealed that his tumour was cancerous, and he was rushed straight into surgery. When he woke up, the prognosis was good. His doctor was confident that he'd removed the whole tumour, and Richard was elated. He'd kicked cancer's ass. A few weeks later he started routine radiation, and three weeks after that a follow-up MRI revealed the cancer had spread – and that's when Richard was told he had six months left to live.

CHANGE YOUR THINKING, CHANGE YOUR LIFE

Richard admits that he was angry with his prognosis, but mainly at his doctors for putting a timeline on his life. 'Who were they to define that for me?' he said. 'Did they know who they were speaking to? I was an Ironman athlete.'

And in a way, Richard was right. He was the least likely candidate for terminal cancer – which also made him the best candidate to overcome it, if he could get his mindset right, which at first, he couldn't.

'When you find out you have cancer, here's what I learned: You will try anything in the faint hope that it's a cure. Anything. My life became about beating my cancer. And because of that, I became a victim of cancer.'

How often do we see this in entrepreneurship: I'm a victim of my market. I'm a victim of a poor economy, or red tape. How often do we fixate on the issues? Richard calls it the cancer in our marketplace, and as entrepreneurs, we're all guilty of it.

There are two key lessons that Richard was able to share with me because of his experience, which he shares when he gives motivational talks and with the business owners he consults with.

The first is that our brains are the most sophisticated filtration systems on the planet. We are always automatically making judgements, and yet our brains can't think for themselves. They do what we tell them to do – they operate on the thoughts that we put in.

'We jump to snap – often negative – conclusions, and then we look for reasons to validate those thoughts. It's a vicious cycle,' he said. 'The problem is that our thoughts are the only things in life we have 100% control over, and yet they're the thing we are worst at controlling.'

'I was a cancer victim – my whole life was about cancer – how bad my marketplace was, and how I needed to find a cure for it. I was focusing on the problem. The cancer. I wasn't focusing on the solution – me.'

In his sixth week of radiation and feeling terrible, Richard fetched his two daughters from school. It was his week, and he would never move his time to see them, but he was struggling – and visibly so. Instead of quietly pretending that everything was fine, his daughter said to him, 'Daddy, nobody said it would be easy.'

It was a sentence that would change everything for Richard. 'I don't know where she heard that, but it snapped something in me. If you want to get through this thing, I realised, if you want to make it through to the other side, then something has to change. Because no, it's not easy. But you want to survive.'

'So, that's where I started. How can I start overcoming this, instead of feeding it? Well, how had I overcome everything in my life? I did the Ironman. I trained. I poured everything I had into physical activity.'

Richard was the first amateur finisher at his first Ironman, and sixteenth overall. It's a remarkable achieve-ment, and yet he isn't the fastest swimmer, runner or cyclist. He doesn't compete against everyone else though; he only competes with himself. 'You don't need to be the best at everything,' he said. 'The fourth discipline in Ironman is the mental side. It's so easy to end up competing against others, and when you do that, you lose.' Richard's strength lies in his endurance. He has an incredible capacity for perseverance. He breaks down whatever he's doing into smaller goals, and then just starts. That's the secret – getting started.

'That night, I put out my running shoes and set my alarm. Even if I walked, I was getting up. My training was starting. If you can develop the grit, the tenacity, the determination – whatever it is that you need to motivate yourself – and then make a habit of it, you'll do it. You can change everything. You just need to start by changing your thinking.'

And this was Richard's second big lesson: The power of living the most authentic version of yourself and your life. 'I went back to what makes me feel good. I found my authentic place – who I am. Because, believe me, it's hard to be resilient if you aren't authentic. When the chips are down, what is your Ironman? What will change your life?'

The key to this lesson is that you can't change something long-lasting through behaviour. You have to change your thinking. Impactful change (and we all want to change something – who we are, our businesses, results, sales teams) comes when we change how we think about things, and yet we always focus on behaviour instead of mindset and thoughts.

'I see it time and time again,' said Richard. 'Businesses try to change behaviours through the KPIs they set, their focus areas and goalposts that move and shift. The problem is that it's all meaningless unless your team figures out their identity. Who are you? Why are you doing what you're doing?'

In my own experience, I've realised that in the entrepreneurial space, we often end up fixated *on* the business. I'm guilty of it too, but the really successful entrepreneurs I know manage to extricate themselves from their businesses. They own successful companies, but they aren't slaves to them. They're focused on more.

This resonated with me in terms of what Richard was sharing. We all know that goals are important, but they need to be authentic goals that speak to our values and our why.

If you just want to be the biggest player, to land that client, that office – good luck to you. If you aren't starting with the best version of yourself, or with your why, it's unlikely you'll feel successful, even if you do achieve all of those things.

The problem is that we are programmed to be negative. It's evolutionary. 'There are seven *Homos*, and we, *Homo sapiens*, are the only ones that survived,' said Richard. 'Not because we're the fastest or the strongest. We survived because we defended ourselves. Our babies can't even survive on their own. Our first response is a negative one because we're programmed to see danger. We fear the unknown – but fear can help you survive, or it can paralyse you.'

It's the choice Richard faced: cancer victim or cancer survivor?

'I have cancer now. It's come back three times. I'm having chemotherapy again. But I learned after the first time that you don't need to be in remission to be a survivor. I'm surviving right now. Every day that cancer hasn't taken me is another day that I've survived. We're all surviving something and we should celebrate that. Don't wait until you've reached some goalpost to celebrate. Live now. If you do, your mindset will change.'

Richard goes on to say, 'It doesn't matter what the market's doing, what your buyers are doing, what the competition is doing, or even what the economy is doing. None of that matters. I control my universe and it begins with my thoughts.'

He adds, 'Yes, we're genetically programmed to be negative. But we also control our own thoughts. What we think is powerful, so make sure it's the right thing. What you tell yourself on a daily basis will determine everything.'

WHAT COLONEL SANDERS CAN TEACH US ABOUT GRIT

History is littered with stories of incredible perseverance, and most of the brands we know and love today wouldn't exist without it.

The link between grit, perseverance and success stands particularly true in the case of Harland David Sanders. Sanders was born in 1890 in Henryville, Indiana. When he was six years old, his father passed away, leaving Sanders to cook and care for his siblings. In seventh grade, he dropped out of school and left home to work as a farmhand. At 16, he faked his age to enlist in the United States army. After being honourably discharged a year later, he got hired by the railway as a labourer, but was soon fired for fighting with a co-worker. While he worked for the railway, he studied law – until he ruined his legal career by getting into another fight. Sanders was forced to move back in with his mom and get a job selling life insurance. And guess what? He got fired for insubordination. But just like Richard Wright, and countless other success stories, this guy just wouldn't give up. He chose to persevere.

In 1920, he founded a ferry boat company. Later, he tried cashing in his ferry boat business to create a lamp manufacturing company, only to find out that another company already sold a better version of his lamp. The poor guy couldn't catch a break. It wasn't until age 40 that he began selling chicken dishes at a service station. As he began to advertise his food, an argument with a competitor resulted in a deadly shootout. Four years later, he bought a motel that burned to the ground, along with his restaurant. He still didn't quit. He rebuilt and ran a new motel, until World War II forced him to close it down.

Following the war, Sanders finally managed to build a successful restaurant until it was crippled by an interstate opening nearby. Instead of giving up, he sold the restaurant and concentrated on his secret recipe chicken. His recipe was rejected 1 009 times (just stop and imagine that for a second) before anyone accepted it.

If you haven't guessed by now, that 'secret recipe' is the very same recipe that would catapult Kentucky Fried Chicken to international success for decades to come.

Sanders' dream was to franchise Kentucky Fried Chicken and open stores across the country. After years of failures and misfortunes, the Colonel finally hit it big. KFC expanded internationally and Sanders sold the company for $2 million (about $17 million today). Decades later, he remains central in KFC's branding and his face still appears in its logo. His goatee, white suit and western string tie continue to symbolise delicious country-fried chicken all over the world.

At age 90, the Colonel passed away from pneumonia. At that time, there were around 6 000 KFC locations in 48 countries. As of year-end 2018, there are 23 000 KFC outlets in 119 countries and territories across the world.

It's a story from decades ago, but what I love about it is the fact that Sanders only found success in his forties. Nothing is instant. Success takes time. Because the Colonel's story began almost 100 years ago, some people don't believe it's still relevant today – that the world has changed too much. I disagree. He spent decades not giving up. It was a muscle that he worked and worked and worked – and his brand is still an international giant today as a result. We can learn a lot from that level of determination.

Angela Duckworth, a psychologist and the author of the best-selling book, *Grit: The Power of Passion and Perseverance*, spent years trying to identify the key factor that defines success. She started studying kids and adults in all kinds of super-challenging settings, and in every study her question was, who is successful here and why?

Her research team went to West Point Military Academy and tried to predict which cadets would stay in military training and which would drop out. They went to the National Spelling Bee and tried to predict which children would advance furthest in competitions.

They studied rookie teachers working in tough neighbourhoods, asking which teachers were still going to be there by the end of the school year, and who would be the most effective at improving their students' learning outcomes. They partnered with private companies, asking which of their sales people would keep their jobs? And who would earn the most money?

In all those different contexts, one characteristic emerged as a significant predictor of success, and it wasn't social intelligence. It wasn't good looks, physical health or IQ. It was grit.

Grit is passion and perseverance for very long-term goals. It's having stamina and sticking to your goals, day in and day out, not just for a week or a month, but for years. It's looking at the future you want and working hard to make that future a reality. Grit is living life like it's a marathon, not a sprint.

Duckworth believes the most shocking thing about grit is how little we know about it. Science can't tell us how we build it. All Duckworth and her team do know is that talent doesn't make you gritty. Their data shows that many talented individuals do not follow through on their commitments. In fact, grit is usually unrelated or even inversely related to measures of talent.

So, how can we foster grit in ourselves as entrepreneurs? Dr Carol Dweck, a professor at Stanford University, has developed an idea that centres on something called 'growth mindset', which basically says that the ability to learn is not fixed; that it can change with your effort. Dr Dweck has shown that when kids read and learn about the brain and how it changes and grows in response to challenges, they're more likely to persevere when they fail, *because they don't believe that failure is permanent*.

Imagine that. Understanding that failure isn't permanent and that we can persevere *helps us build grit*. This was a revelation to me. It's not just something we're born with – we can build it within ourselves. I realised that I'd personally done this when I pulled myself back from my first failure. This is at the core of how entrepreneurs like Allon have used failure to motivate greater success. They work at it. Every entrepreneur I've ever interviewed has had grit in spades. Without it, you can't build an Inner Game that will lead to success.

PAIN, PERSEVERANCE AND REGRET

Pain is never a reason to quit. If you've started a business, you're familiar with a particular kind of pain that all startup entrepreneurs have experienced. If you're a mature, profitable company with product market fit, you're just experiencing different kinds of pain. Even billionaires are familiar with pain. No matter who you are, or what the size of your business is, there will always be some form of pain that you have to deal with.

Pain points are problems, challenges and issues that entrepreneurs and businesses are dealing with on a daily basis. These pain points can be materialistic (no cash flow, no runway, no revenue), or idealistic (you hate your business, you don't feel appreciated, you're confused about your motivations... the list goes on). But regardless of the pain you're personally experiencing in your business, there is no excuse to quit on your dream. If you quit at anything, you automatically fail. Whenever I even think about quitting anything, I think back to Joey Evans' words: 'I didn't get this far to only get this far.' It gets me in the mindset that I need to be in, a mindset that allows me to say, 'Screw that, there's no way I'm quitting now. Bring on the pain.'

All of my business failures were a direct result of my decision to quit. This is one of the biggest regrets of my business career. I spend a lot of time wondering 'what if?' What if I raised the money to fund the rest of the R&D for the Kidmogo tracking bracelet instead of giving up? What if I pivoted Animus Potential? What if I did this? What if I did that? What if I never quit? These two words are always the precursor to the worst kind of regret. This is why grit and discipline really matter, and why I've consciously focused on building both within myself.

True grit is making a decision and then sticking to it, despite the pain you might be experiencing at the time. Discipline is doing what needs to be done when you don't want to do it. The two go hand in hand. It's easy to do anything when things are easy. But if you want to build a successful business, you have to make a choice every single day: Suffer the pain of discipline or suffer the pain of regret.

THREE FEET FROM GOLD

In his all-time classic book, *Think and Grow Rich*, Napoleon Hill recounts the story of R.U. Darby. It was the 1800s during the gold rush. Darby's uncle was caught up in the gold fever, and so Darby staked his own claim and started digging. After months of hard work, they had not struck gold. Then one day, Darby's uncle found a vein of ore. To mine the gold he needed to raise the working capital required to move the gold to the surface, and so he returned home to raise the money for the machinery he needed. It was the height of the gold fever, so Darby and his uncle had no trouble finding funders.

They soon returned to the site and began mining the ore. As luck would have it, this particular vein of ore was one of the biggest ever discovered during the gold rush and for months they mined huge gold deposits. But then one day, the supply of gold stopped. The vein of ore had just disappeared. They kept digging, but found nothing. Eventually, all the money that they had invested into the mine was gone. In frustration, they quit and sold their machinery to a junk man for a few hundred dollars, returning home broke and disappointed.

These 'junk men' were hustlers and street traders. They were not regarded as particularly savvy or intelligent. This particular junk man, however, had heard the story of the

Darbys. He decided to call in a mining engineer and asked him to check the plans of the mine to see what had gone wrong. How could such a large vein of ore just disappear? Two weeks later, the engineer came back to him with two key findings. First, the Darbys were idiots. Second, by his calculations, they were three feet away from rediscovering the vein of gold. But they had stopped digging. Literally, three feet. Needless to say, that junk man went on to make millions from the mine. If only the Darbys had not given up. All they needed to do was dig three more feet (and maybe do some research).

I love this story. It sums up what happens when you give up on your dream. If you ever feel like quitting, just remember the Darbys.

WHEN TO QUIT YOUR BUSINESS

Stories like that of Richard Wright, Joey Evans and even the Colonel himself are great inspiration for when you're in the doldrums. But I also acknowledge that there comes a time when throwing in the towel is in fact the best choice for you as an entrepreneur.

Over the years I've received numerous messages from my listeners, asking for help in answering the following question: When should I quit my business? I've found this simple framework to be helpful, and it's based on the following two questions:

1) Are you in love with the vision?

2) Is your business making money?

If you are still in love with the vision but your business is not making money, then fix the business problem. If your business is making money and you are not in love with the vision, then you should question why, but don't quit. However, if your business is not making money and you are not in love with the vision, then it is probably time to consider throwing in the towel.

Whether you choose to quit or push through, remember that building a business is supposed to be hard. If it wasn't, everyone would be doing it. There is no timeline to success, or expiration date when it comes to facing – and surviving – challenges. It doesn't magically get easier. The challenges just change, and you get better at dealing with them.

You just have to keep going until it pays off. Or quit. But if you do decide to quit, I would urge you to ask a few hard questions before you do: What are you going to do if you do throw in the towel? Are you willing to forego the independence of working for yourself for a steady job and pay-cheque with less freedom? Is what you are feeling the result of short-term fatigue? Finally, can you just take a step back and get rested?

Saying goodbye to a business can be an emotional and conflicting journey. So, if you are in doubt, leave it out – there is no excuse to ever quit on your dreams while there's still breath in your body – unless the dream has changed. The key is not to be afraid of the uncertainties of the future. Nothing is certain. That's what makes entrepreneurship so exciting – and so full of possibilities.

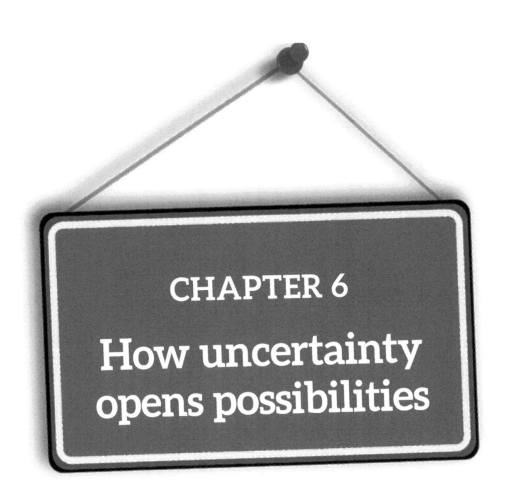

CHAPTER 6

How uncertainty
opens possibilities

Player:	**Ian Fuhr,** Founder and CEO Sorbet
Episode:	MBS129
Principle:	*I will embrace uncertainty*

Trust the wait. Embrace the uncertainty. When nothing is certain, anything is possible.

– MANDY HALE

*I*t was 2004. Ian Fuhr had just sold his business, Super Mart, to the Edcon Group. While lying on a massage table one day, having a think about what his next entrepreneurial play was going to be, his beauty therapist said: 'Why don't you consider going into the beauty industry?'

He thought she was joking. He didn't know anything about beauty. 'I used some Lux soap once or twice a week and that was about it. The sum total of my beauty regime,' he stated.

'I used to think a Brazilian was someone from Brazil and that a Hollywood was a place where they made movies,' he joked. 'I also never understood what it was about women and their nails, because when I'm at a braai and a beautiful woman walks past, I've never heard a bunch of guys say "wow, look at those incredible nails!"'

But the question stuck with him, enough that he started doing some research. It soon became apparent that not only was the local beauty industry very fragmented, but on the whole, it was also incredibly unprofessional. Ian and his business partner, Rudi Rudolph, discussed their options. They both came from a retail background, and they decided that perhaps there was a way to enter the beauty industry with a professional offering that also had a retail arm, combining what they knew with new territory.

And so, the first Sorbet beauty salon opened its doors. Right out of the gates the business was a struggle. 'We call them the "dark days",' said Ian, referring to the first four years of the business. The partners had managed to open 22 stores, but no matter what they tried, they couldn't seem to franchise the business, which was their big growth play.

On top of that, after investing R19 million into the venture, the business still hadn't turned a profit. Think about it: You build a successful business, sell it and then sink R19 million into a new venture that after four years still hasn't turned a profit. By that stage, I'd be ill over the uncertainty of what I was doing – and why. There comes a time when you just need to cut your losses and move on (yes, there are sometimes good reasons to quit, but clearly this wasn't one of them, or Sorbet wouldn't exist today).

Displaying his own hard-won grit and perseverance, Ian didn't choose that route. A seasoned entrepreneur, he had overcome his fear and uncertainty way back in 1986, when a business he was running had gone insolvent. Ian was sequestrated by the courts and for four long years could not even open a bank account.

'I've always believed that that was probably my best learning experience by far. The failure itself, as well as understanding why the business failed and how you're going to fix it the next time, are all invaluable. Success is not always reachable unless you've failed at least once and lost everything.'

What I love about Ian's attitude is how he looked at the failure through the eyes of how he would fix things the next time. I discuss re-entry rate in Chapter 4, and Ian is a perfect example of an entrepreneur who doesn't fit the South African average of a 1.1 re-entry rate. He's enjoyed success because he's willing – and able – to learn from failure, pick himself up and try again.

He went on to say, 'If you haven't failed, don't have a fear of failure, or cannot deal with the uncertainty that goes with running a business, it's unlikely that you'll ever become a great entrepreneur.' I couldn't agree more.

SOLVING SORBET'S ITCH WITH A CREATIVE SCRATCH

The scaling challenge that Sorbet faced was twofold. First, the brand lacked the most elusive of traits: Credibility. Too late, Ian and Rudi realised that their name sounded like an ice cream parlour instead of a beauty salon (hard to imagine today).

Second, to scale an in-store experience in a consistent fashion was proving to be a massive challenge. 'It's hard to create a consistent customer experience in one store, and we were operating over twenty stores,' he says. To replicate the experience, Ian focused on design and culture. Across all stores, treatment rooms were moved to the back of the premises and branded retail fronts and service desks installed. But most importantly, the secret ingredient came down to the culture of the business itself.

'The culture of our organisation has always been a focus on people and service rather than money. Once you get that right, the money comes. It seems so obvious and, yet, often the focus on results persists and people get lost in the wash. The most important group of people in Sorbet are our staff. Without them, we can't be successful. Our core value is "servant leadership", which basically means always putting our customers first. But to do that, we need to put our staff first, and then they pay it forward.'

Here's how servant leadership works. First, Ian personally conducts all induction training. 'My focus isn't on what you do or how you do it, but rather *why* you do it. Our staff need to believe that we're not selling treatments and products. We're selling a feeling. People want to feel good about themselves, and that's what we give them.'

Interestingly, once Ian and Rudi started concentrating on building a brand reputation and credibility, franchisees followed, many of whom started out as customers who loved the brand and then enquired about potentially owning a franchise themselves.

Fast forward to today, and Sorbet employs over 3 000 staff, has over 200 stores (which deliver a staggering 350 000 individual beauty treatments a month). Sorbet receives 40 franchise applications per week. Demand is so high that new locations are the biggest challenge for the 15-year-old business.

To cope with the ever-growing interest in the brand, from both consumers and prospective franchisees, new concepts have been launched, like Candi & Co, Sorbet Man, and Sorbet Dry Bars. It's hard to imagine that just a few short years ago, Ian Fuhr was unable to sell a single franchise.

HOW TO OVERCOME UNCERTAINTY

The story of Sorbet is one largely about dealing with uncertainty as an entrepreneur and what can be achieved when you understand that your tolerance for uncertainty is the prerequisite to succeeding at building a scale business.

When it comes to business, there is virtually nothing certain but the uncertain. Feeling unsure and lost is pretty much part and parcel of the entrepreneurial journey; it's virtually impossible to avoid feelings of doubt and fear as a business owner. But here's the thing about uncertainty: You will not win the fight against uncertainty by becoming certain; instead your certainty will come as a result of embracing uncertainty.

All entrepreneurs are, at their core, a little crazy. They see things that no one else sees and ultimately, whether they're right or wrong, it's not going to stop them from pursuing that vision. It's an important character trait though, because when you go out there, you're not just selling your product, business or even vision – you're selling yourself.

Entrepreneurs basically spend all of their time convincing other people to take a leap of faith with them – partners, employees, customers and even suppliers. Everyone becomes a part of the journey. Entrepreneurship is risky – and with that risk comes a bucket-load of fear and doubt. If you can't overcome that fear – or at least harness it – a scale business will not lie in your future.

Jerry Seinfeld once said that success is the enemy of comedy. What he meant was that once you have a routine that you know makes people laugh, you think you've eliminated uncertainty. So, if you come onto a stage and you do that routine again and again, and again and again and again, you'll continue to get laughs. Except we all know that's bullshit, because you're not the only comedian out there that's trying to get laughs. The idea that doing something over and over and over again will provide you with a level of certainty is a complete illusion. There is nothing about the future that's certain. The only thing that's certain for all of us is death.

Anyone who tells you that they know what's going to happen six months, or a year from now, is just talking rubbish. There are no certainties. No one knows what's going to happen next. This is the most dynamic world we've ever lived in. You can't control everything that happens, so focus instead on yourself: are you living your life as fully and as passionately as you can?

Be careful though, don't fall into that trap of 'Do what you love and the money will follow'. That's bullshit too. How about do what you love and you'll love what you do. That's an interesting one. It makes sense mathematically too, since there's no guarantee – ever – that doing something will lead to riches. Live your life the way you want to live your life. Because it's no one else's life and everything that anyone thinks about you and what you're doing and your choices is irrelevant. If you can make money from it, great. If you can't, do what you love as a hobby and find something else to pay the bills.

When it comes to uncertainty, you can't be afraid to fail, otherwise you won't be able to make the tough decisions. You have to have a sense that it is right, even if you don't have the evidence yet to prove it.

I'll leave you with this final thought. Uncertainty is a given, but it can also be an opportunity. No one knows what's going to happen, which means if you can conquer your fear of uncertainty you can harness it and provide solutions that at least offer some degree of certainty for your customers.

Ian and Rudi leapt into an industry that was completely new to them. They included a retail element in their business model, which helped, but ultimately they embraced uncertainty, used their wits, refused to quit when things didn't go quite as planned and built an iconic South African brand as a result.

CHAPTER 7

Beliefs that others
can follow

Player:	**Tom Asacker,** international best-selling author
Episode:	MBS072 and MBS105
Principle:	*I believe in my mission*

A belief is not merely an idea of the mind, it is an idea that possesses the mind.

– ROBERT BOLTON

*T*om Asacker is the author of five critically acclaimed books: *The Business of Belief, Opportunity Screams, A Little Less Conversation* and *A Clear Eye for Branding*; all ground-breaking books that unpack new practices, frameworks and ideas for success in times of uncertainty and change.

His first book, *Sandbox Wisdom*, is a heart-warming story about a CEO's search for meaning and success in the world of business. When I first interviewed Tom, we discussed the business of belief and how entrepreneurs can use it to build great businesses, but at the same time stay true to themselves and, ultimately, their happiness.

During our interview, Tom recounted an incredible story about belief from his time as the president of a startup medical device company. The company had developed a product that could help people with nocturnal hyperventilation, which basically means they weren't breathing deeply enough during sleep, one of the leading causes of sleep apnoea.

He was presenting at a teaching hospital in the United States to the leading physicians in the world who were involved in studying the disorder. The meeting had been arranged by a sales rep who sold the product through a distribution company.

It was a lunchtime meeting, so Tom had brought sandwiches for everyone, and he was at the front of the room with an overhead projector and clear pieces of plastic that you write on. At noon the doctors entered. They were all dressed in their physician's scrubs and they had their stethoscopes dangling around their necks. They sat down, opened up their sandwiches and looked at the documents in front of them, which were the results of clinical trials that Tom's company had done with the device. He was there to explain those trials and how well the patients involved had responded to them.

What happened next will be familiar to many entrepreneurs, even if the details differ. Tom took all the doctors in the room through the entire presentation, and when he reached the end, one of the leading physicians in the world just sat there, staring at him (for any entrepreneur who has pitched for funding, this is pretty much your worst nightmare).

The physician said: 'Mr Asacker, can I ask you a question?' Tom said sure, expecting a technical question. He believed he was ready to answer anything thrown at him. But instead he was asked, 'Mr Asacker, as the president of the company, how can you come to my teaching hospital with such shoddy data?' Tom's heart was racing. He hadn't been prepared for that. He looked around the room and saw that a few of the faces felt bad for him. He knew that if he walked out of that room right then and there, it was all over. He'd never get his device into hospitals or the endorsements of medical professionals. The 30 people employed in his manufacturing facility would be out of jobs. The business would be finished. He was thinking at the speed of light.

On the one hand, the worst was busy happening. On the other, he knew the data was good. He had gone to one of the most reputable teaching institutions in the country to get that data. He realised that big medical companies which could spend tens of millions of dollars studying thousands of patients could get *more* data, but that didn't mean it was *better* data. They were a startup that couldn't afford to spend that kind of money, so they'd done the bare minimum required by the FDA to pass approval of the device. With all this buzzing through his head, Tom's inner *belief* in his product and spirit took over. He threw caution to the wind because he knew he didn't have anything to lose.

Instead of apologising about the quality of his data, or even trying to explain where it had been sourced or why it was based on so few patients, he said instead: 'Doctor, do me a favour. Turn to patient ten.' He opened the document in front of him, which was full of squiggly lines, physiological readings like oxygen saturation levels. To preserve patient confidentiality there was no name on the data. And Tom said, 'Doctor do you see those squiggly lines?' 'Squiggly lines' is not a medical term you would usually use with a doctor, but Tom was upset.

'Those squiggly lines are Jim Olson. Jim Olson lives in a little white house with a beautiful little picket fence, two adorable little girls that love their father, and a wife that adores her husband. No product in the marketplace could help Jim Olson. Our product saved Jim Olson's life. So, if the minute squiggly lines and data mean more to you than people's lives, well that's the day you should get out of medicine.' At this point, Tom pointed to all the other doctors in the room and said, 'You should all get out of medicine.' And with that, he picked up his stuff and walked away, sweat pouring down his back. Tom thought his company was over.

Instead, something magical happened. That same physician, who until that point had never sat on a medical company's board because he didn't want a conflict of interest, phoned Tom and told him that he would sit on his company's board of advisors. That's how much of an impact Tom's belief in his product had had on that room full of doctors. From that point forward, Tom was a rock star, because he was the guy who had told some of the leading physicians in the country that if they cared more about numbers than people's lives, they should get out of medicine. And he earned huge respect for that.

THE BUSINESS OF BELIEF

Tom Asacker's book, *The Business of Belief*, unpacks how the world's best marketers, designers, salespeople, entrepreneurs, fundraisers, educators and leaders essentially get us to believe in what they're doing. For entrepreneurs in particular, if you're going to scale a business, you better be damn sure that your best asset – your people – believe in what you're building. Otherwise, that plane is going to fall apart mid-air.

Tom wrote this book because he became frustrated working with organisations that were trying to get people to move one way, but without performance measures that supported the vision. In other words, the rhetoric and the reality were miles apart.

The final blow was a visit to a CEO whom he'd spent a week with 12 months earlier. He'd returned to review their progress, and not only had they made none, but they were doing almost the exact opposite of what he had recommended. When he asked the CEO what he had done wrong, or what they disagreed with in his methodology, the CEO candidly said, 'Nothing Tom. But remember, when you left people had to go back to their jobs.'

This struck Tom as a profoundly interesting statement. What he was discovering was that knowledge doesn't make people change their behaviour. You can fill people with as much knowledge as you want and it won't amount to anything. In fact, you'll be wasting your time. What moves people is their personal desires. So, if people don't have the desire for whatever it is that you're hoping for them to adopt, whether it's an idea, a product, a service-ethos, whatever it is, if they don't have a personal desire for it, then they are simply not going to do it. Beliefs are driven by desires. They are *not* driven by knowledge.

What does this mean for the business owner? If you're not tapping into people's desires, from your employees to your customers, or your partners, then there's nothing you can say or do that will get them to come along for the ride. You can try, but you'll end up like Tom, spending 20 years getting frustrated before you figure out why people don't change.

Belief is a desire that's driven by a wish. So, to have a belief you have to have a wish for something in the future. Otherwise, why change what you're doing right now? There needs to be a driving force that says you think you're going to improve something or build something of value. With this in mind, Tom shared his 'rickety bridge' metaphor of belief with me.

What is the one thing that will get you across a rickety bridge spanning a deep chasm? This is what you have to cross to achieve your intended outcome. It's scary, possibly dangerous, definitely a challenge.

So, what's on the other side? What's pulling you? As you start stepping across that bridge, you're looking for evidence that tells you that the bridge is safe and that it makes sense to keep walking across it. Without something compelling on the other side, you're not going to take the risk.

Now consider what happens when you're working with customers or employees – you're taking them to a place of change, and they're looking for fear signals – anything that tells them they shouldn't be braving the bridge. Any opening and they'll get off that bridge, particularly given the amount of choice we are inundated with today.

If you want to change someone's behaviour or lead them over that bridge, you need to show them you can improve their life. You need to show them that the bridge is safe. You need an inspiring message that turns on their feelings for whatever it is that you're offering. Once that gets turned on, their rational mind comes along for the ride and starts looking for trouble to make sure this bridge is safe.

How you handle this has a lot to do with what you're selling. If you're selling something like a bottle of wine that anyone can pick up at the supermarket, you have to know how to appeal to their aesthetic taste. How do you give them control over the purchase? How do you make the pricing such that their identity is in line with what they're picking up? There's far less risk associated with trying a new bottle of wine compared to adopting a new software system. Ask someone to change their religious beliefs, or vote for a new political party. These are near impossible tasks. That's how huge the role of belief is in our choices and our identities.

Ask someone to do something that's really tied to their sense of self and their story, and if they find anything that seems even slightly unsafe or unstable, they will tune it out and walk away from it. The more you understand this, the more you can address it – in yourself as well.

It's incredibly important to understand the step-by-step process of how influence and belief are created so that you don't derail yourself without even realising it.

Most executives and entrepreneurs have said some version of this sentence: 'The customer just doesn't understand that our offering is better. We have to give them more information. They just don't get it.'

Here's the secret: They're not interested in your information. They want the easiest and safest path to the future that they're envisioning for themselves and their businesses. They don't want any stress. They don't want to waste time. They want you to get them there, and if you can do that, they'll come along with you. But if you can't do that, or if they don't trust in the process, they'll just walk away. People are always going to do whatever is easiest for them; or what they think is going to give them the best experience while supporting their story about themselves. All beliefs are just the foundation of the story we craft around ourselves.

That's the next paradox – as entrepreneurs with ambitions of scaling, we need to go out into the marketplace and forget our own stories. We need to be scientists, experimenting with what does and doesn't work in the marketplace. We need to figure out everyone else's stories and tap into those, forgetting our own.

Always remember that all the entrepreneurial greats whom we admire so much also had to go out into the market and improvise. They also didn't know what they were doing. Jeff Bezos didn't know he would one day start making movies. He was just trying to sell books. But because he was out experimenting, he made discoveries, shifted direction, tried new things and redeployed resources. He wasn't afraid to go out there and do it. Nothing gave him the right to do anything. He gave it to himself.

If we relate this to Inner Game, the principle is deceptively simple: if you don't believe in yourself and your mission, how will you ever convince anyone else to believe in it? You need to start with yourself, really interrogate what your mission is, and most importantly, conquer your self-limiting beliefs.

DEBUGGING LIMITING BELIEFS

One of the most compelling truths I've learned about success in business is that the only thing that stops you from getting what you want is the story you keep telling yourself about why you can't have it. This story is either going to make building a successful, purposeful business possible for you, or it will only serve to reinforce it as a pipe dream.

Here's the thing; you can only grow a business to the extent that you grow yourself, which means it's important to foster a strong growth mindset right from day one. One of the greatest gifts you can give yourself as an entrepreneur is to carry out a fearless and moral inventory of your limiting beliefs, because these are what determine your own inner narrative and ultimately, this narrative controls your life, whether you choose to admit it or not. Henry Ford said it best: 'Whether you think you can or you can't, you're right.'

Here's the problem. Limiting beliefs sit underneath the surface of our conscious minds. They determine whether we're going to dent the universe or whether the universe will put a dent in us. In my own personal case, I almost didn't start podcasting. I'm an introvert who doesn't like strangers. I never have. I'd much rather hang out with people I know *and* like. In the early days of podcasting, I remember very clearly how excruciatingly painful it was to sit down with a 'stranger CEO' for an hour, holding a conversation. There couldn't be any awkward moments or silent pauses either. It had to flow, it had to sound natural, and most importantly, I needed to sound like I was enjoying myself.

When I launched *The Matt Brown Show*, I had plenty of experience in business and a lot of self-confidence; I just hated the idea of talking to a stranger and everything being recorded – essentially, being a prisoner to my own words live on air. A limiting belief was at play, I just didn't realise it at first.

Imagine this: I'd be interviewing someone in the same city – even suburb – as myself, and I'd still do a Skype interview. I didn't invite my guest into studio with me. It took a little while, but I eventually realised how completely ridiculous the entire situation was. It was almost farcical. I knew I needed to figure out why I reacted to strangers in this way. Turns out there were two factors that combined when I started my show. The first is one we're all familiar with – stranger danger, driven into us when we're kids.

The second was more personal. I used to have a huge fear of public speaking. Turns out, buried in my subconscious was a massive limiting belief of being judged by my peers. In essence, I was terrified of saying the wrong thing, being judged by my peers, and consequently not worthy of their love or respect. How messed up is that?

If I hadn't managed to overcome that limiting belief, I would have never been able to pull off an event like #CryptoTrader – a live show in front of 600 people and broadcast in real-time to a live audience in over 52 countries around the world.

So much of what we believe and operate on stems from our past, and we just let it sit there instead of facing it. We never take the time to deal with it. It's all fine and well to talk about scale and chasing the big things, focusing on our goals and wanting to 10x our businesses, but none of that is achievable if we don't face our own inner reality.

There are so many pressures and stresses that impact our lives and abilities as human beings, and our ability to build something of purpose and meaning is tied up in them. If you want to build a successful business, whether that's a business of scale or a lifestyle business, you need to face them. You need to figure out what's happening below the surface, because you, like me, are a product of your experiences. Like the stranger danger example these can sit beneath the surface of your consciousness for years, manifesting in behaviours that can cripple your ability to execute to your fullest potential.

If we're all able to be brutally honest with ourselves, as well as introspective, I believe each of us will find an internal limiting belief linked to self-worth. We have to face these. If you hate the idea of cold-calling, then you probably have a limiting belief that affects your ability to call complete strangers and pitch yourself, business or product to them.

If you have a limiting belief about your ability to compete toe-to-toe with the best entrepreneurs in the world, you need to recognise it so that you can address it. Unfortunately, most of us let these kinds of limiting beliefs run in the background, putting the destination of our lives on autopilot. But, if you have the courage to explore it, you'll start tugging on one piece of the string and the rest will begin to unravel. Therefore, the question becomes do you have the courage to come to terms with yourself? How open are you to overcoming your greatest fears; your fear of not being good enough? How open are you to losing it all in the pursuit of building a global brand and business?

How open are you to experimenting, to trying, failing and trying again?

In case you think I'm making this all up, there's a very real syndrome that most entrepreneurs struggle with at one time or another. It's called Impostor Syndrome. In a nutshell, Impostor Syndrome is a psychological pattern in which we doubt our accomplishments, coupled with a persistent internalised fear of being exposed as a fraud.

I was suffering from Impostor Syndrome before I started writing this book. I knew the lessons I wanted to share and the value of those lessons – for myself personally, but also the people who have been listening to my show for over four years. There's so much we can learn from each other. But I was still paralysed by doubt and fear.

And then I remembered that I had been through this before. It's not a once-off that we can face, get over and move on. It's a process. Mainly, it's about getting to the truth instead of just buying in to the fear. I also remembered my original mission with *The Matt Brown Show* – helping entrepreneurs and business leaders succeed through information sharing at scale. This book is just an extension of that.

There are two techniques I use daily to help me get to the truth of any challenge I am facing, or a solution to a problem I am thinking about. The first is reflection through meditation. Reflection is one of the most underrated, yet powerful tools for success as an entrepreneur. Reflection helps us get to the truth of our individual experiences, because we do not learn from the experience itself, we learn from *reflecting* on our experiences. Journaling and meditation are proven ways to help provide clarity on the lessons being taught to us as we scale our businesses. Whatever we don't reflect upon is usually not learned from or retained.

Because the human mind does an awesome job at distorting, generalising and deleting information, the second technique I use is called triangulation. This is a method I've developed that helps me avoid the distorted and false view I have of my own reality and instead get to the heart of any matter. I take matter X and ask three other people their opinion.

Let's say I wanted to pivot Digital Kungfu away from technology businesses and focus solely on offering a personal branding service to entrepreneurs. I'm all gung-ho about the idea but I have no evidence to prove that my new shiny pivot idea is going to work. To get to the truth, I need to bring other views into my own perspective and so I call three other people in my network to get their views. It's important that they feel like they can be completely honest, of course (you shouldn't be looking for a pat on the back). Most people will never tell you that you suck to your face, so make sure you let them know you're looking for their honest opinion, and don't react badly if that opinion doesn't align with your own – you'll never get an honest response again from them if you do that.

These people must be trustworthy, experienced in the thing I'm thinking about and ideally people who I hold in the highest regard. Inevitably, if all three views point out that I'm smoking my socks about this pivot idea, then of course I need to bin it and carry on with the business's current direction. But should two of the three suggest pivoting, then my own hypothesis has been validated and therefore the possibility of the idea being a good one can now be put to the test in the real world.

My point is this: If you only ever work with your own model of the world, you're not operating in reality. You need to constantly debug reality and get to the truth. Limiting beliefs are the same. Face them and you'll come out stronger and ready to deal with reality.

THE POWER OF STORY

If people could easily change their inner narrative, there would be no need for psychologists and coaches. But behaviours are a good indication of beliefs. If you aren't investing in your business's growth, even though you know you should, then your own behaviours are telling you something about your true beliefs.

Here's the problem: They may not be true. That's the really interesting thing about beliefs, and it's also incredibly paradoxical – simply believing in something doesn't mean it's true, or even that it's going to happen. The marketplace is advanced. It's an ecosystem. There must be someone else out there that has a strong desire to dance with that same belief that you have.

Tom has experienced this himself. A little over 12 years ago he had the idea that he was going to help revolutionise the radio industry. He was writing for one of the American magazines that dealt with the media industry, and he recognised that if the radio industry didn't start stepping into the digital future – and rapidly – it would be left behind.

He wanted to create a media platform that connected the radio to the Internet as a seamless experience. Because he's not a coder, he needed to find a designer who could help him. He was determined that consumers would love it. He found his designer and together they started building a platform for the radio industry. At one point the designer had it almost completed. Tom had poured a lot of money into the project, and the designer, a kid based in the UK who lived with his mom and coded from her basement, had spent 12 months designing it. Tom said it looked good, but he wanted it to look good on every single browser out there.

The kid was flabbergasted – did Tom know how many browsers were out there? Tom didn't care. He just wanted the kid to figure it out. So, what the kid ended up doing was setting up two computer screens, launching the program in a browser on one screen, looking at it, and making the changes on the other screen. He was going backwards and forwards like this, losing his mind and getting completely frustrated. Then, because of his pain, he said 'wait a minute; why can't I create a computer program that goes out and takes a screenshot of how my web page looks on every browser?' And that's what he did. He built this program to help himself finish Tom's project. He then told some people about it. Turns out, he wasn't the only one feeling that same pain. Someone asked him if they could do that with their emails – take a screenshot, so that they would know what it would look like in client browsers before they sent it out. Based on that, he built a product and then a business and today he's a multi-millionaire.

Tom's product on the other hand was a complete failure. He believed consumers would love it, but he went to the radio industry and they didn't believe they needed it. They thought the Internet was a passing fad. He hadn't gone to the people who needed it, or felt the pain, or even who would love it. That made all the difference in the world. The kid addressed a pain point with the people who needed it solved, and built an empire.

There are a few points to consider here. First, your beliefs won't always be correct. That's as true for your subconscious beliefs as it is for your conscious ones. Be open to new data points and be willing to adjust what you think. Second, personal belief is important, but it's not enough. At the beginning of this chapter we discussed how everyone around you needs to buy into your mission. This is critical. You must find people who either share your belief, or whom you can inspire to get on board. Without that, you're a one-man island.

CHAPTER 8

Without character we have nothing

Player:	**Cathy Davies,** host of *Outpatients – FOX Life*
Episode:	MBS116
Principle:	*I will develop a strong sense of character*

Talent is a gift but character is a choice.

- JOHN MAXWELL

*C*athy Davies is an entrepreneur and a doctor who transforms the lives of ordinary people and celebrities through aesthetic surgery. Through her reality TV show, *Outpatients*, which airs on FOX Life, Cathy shares the real-life stories of ordinary people who have been dealt some unbelievably bad blows. What's truly incredible about their stories though, is that despite everything they share a common trait: The inner strength to push through incredible pain, physical deformities and despair to achieve their dreams.

During my interview with Cathy she recounted a few of the stories that really stood out for her. One, a beautiful 17-year-old Zimbabwean girl called Courtney, was mauled by lions. Another, a talented young rugby player from Port Elizabeth, 'Q', was doused in petrol and set on fire. By the time Cathy met them, they had both almost died and undergone a number of surgeries that had left them heavily scarred and in pain.

Courtney's father owned a game farm in Zimbabwe. There were two lions on the farm, and they'd been brought up to the main house for medical treatment. The lions were kept in an enclosure near the house, as they always were if they needed to be treated in some way. It wasn't a particularly unusual day, except that this time, while Courtney was playing inside the house, the lioness snapped, escaped her enclosure, sprang through the window of the house and pulled Courtney through the burglar bars and back into the enclosure.

The gardener on the property heard screams and growls and went to investigate. What he saw was chilling.

Courtney had somehow managed to escape the lioness's attention and was crawling towards the fence. As she got close, she stood up – and immediately attracted the male lion's attention. He attacked her, seized her in his jaws and pulled her to the ground. The gardener summoned what can only be described as super-human strength and a bucket-load of courage, jumped over the fence and chased the two lions away, picked up Courtney's limp and savaged body and climbed back over the fence.

Courtney was almost dead. She was rushed by helicopter to the nearest hospital and though her life was saved, she was stitched back together so crudely by doctors who lacked the skill to properly deal with her crushed skull. She was eventually moved to Milpark Hospital, where she spent the next few months in the intensive care unit (ICU) recovering from her injuries.

When Cathy first met her, Courtney's eyebrow had been moved right up above the hairline on her forehead. She was a patchwork doll who had suffered both a physical and a mental trauma.

'Q' was a young, talented rugby player at his local school in Port Elizabeth. He'd been scouted by a feeder school and drafted to play for the Blue Bulls, one of the biggest rugby franchises in South Africa. One day, after writing an exam, he was hit on the back of the head by school students with a golf club, doused in petrol and set on fire.

His ears were burned off completely. When he came to, he was still on fire, but managed to run to the nearest tap, begging someone to turn it on so that he could extinguish the flames. He was initially left for dead, but eventually people came to his aid.

Q was flown to Tygerberg Hospital in Cape Town and spent several days in ICU. Months later he was released from hospital. It was at this point that Cathy came into his life. Like Courtney, after several reconstructive surgeries in Dr Cathy's hands, who eventually made a full recovery, Q's scars were repaired and he is even playing rugby again.

He didn't get his scholarship back though – in fact, the incident was never investigated and the principal of the school even claimed that Q had set himself alight. The perpetrators have not been caught.

When Q had recovered enough from his injuries to return to rugby, he emailed the school – not to get his scholarship back, but to get a trial to reclaim his spot on the team with the hope of earning his scholarship again.

The school never replied. What's truly remarkable about this story is that, in spite of everything he's been through, Q holds his head up high. He feels no bitterness and seeks no revenge. Now that's character.

WHEN CHARACTER IS LOST, ALL IS LOST

I find it difficult to imagine the depth of character both Courtney and Q must have to be able to find the strength to overcome the trauma of their experiences. Listening to Cathy recount these stories, I was struck by the fact that both of these events were completely beyond their control.

I've thought about this a lot since first interviewing Cathy. If something goes seriously wrong in your life or business, but it's the result of something that is within your control, that's one thing. Perhaps you learn from it; perhaps you even have the opportunity to fix it, or at least open up new opportunities because of it. But when something goes very wrong as a result of something that is completely beyond your control, that's an entirely different thing.

For me, it would be much more difficult to accept and overcome – particularly if severe mental or physical trauma is experienced. I've discussed these stories countless times, first with Cathy and then with family, friends and other entrepreneurs in my network. I've eventually come to the realisation that when you're faced with a situation that you cannot control – and I'm talking about extreme situations that are fraught with emotions – there's great power in acceptance. By accepting the situation, our life energy is able to flow again, and depression, anxiety or even rage dissipates as the dust settles.

Imagine what it took for Courtney and Q to achieve that level of acceptance. And now imagine if they didn't. Today, they are happy. Without acceptance they would be miserable; trapped in their own existence and past horrors.

These are of course extreme stories – I'm not comparing entrepreneurship to being burned alive or mauled by a lion (not really), but every day we can make the choice to work on what's in our control and accept what's beyond our control, or we can focus on everything that drives us nuts or frustrates us and end up angry and dissatisfied. It's a pretty easy road to take; you just need to sit in Joburg traffic in the morning to know what I'm talking about.

As you pursue your dream of building a business of purpose, there's no magic formula for success except, perhaps, an unconditional acceptance of life and what it brings along your entrepreneurial journey – and making the most of opportunities presented. Sometimes, you're nothing more than an observer; you're looking through a window into other peoples' lives, both positive and negative, thinking you'll never share the same experiences.

We've all thought it: 'That shit will never happen to me.' The challenge is that as entrepreneurs we need to cultivate the ability to truly accept whatever comes and embrace it. If you're going to build a business of significant value you need to develop the habit of looking at whatever happens through a positive mindset instead of a negative, defeatist one.

Acceptance is a choice – a hard one most definitely, but a choice nonetheless. Acceptance is the key to converting momentary happiness into enduring happiness. It helps you move from *feeling* happy to actually *being* happy and believe me, happiness can be a difficult thing to hang onto when you're feeling the pressure of building a business. Finding the lesson or purpose behind every challenge will help you embrace it instead of fight it.

If you believe that everything happens for a reason, better things will always follow. That's the beginning of true acceptance and the seeds of developing a strong character, because when you lose your character you lose everything.

CHAPTER 9

Perfect imperfections

Player: **Brian Altriche**, Founder and CEO
RocoMamas

Episode: MBS128

Principle: *I will embrace my imperfections*

A diamond with a flaw is worth more than a pebble without imperfections.

– PROVERB

O ne of the basic rules of the universe (and entre-preneurship) is that nothing is perfect. Perfection doesn't exist. Ironically, though, we live in a society where social media platforms like Instagram have created an entire subculture that is designed to support the idea of perfection being attainable, and even worse, valuable.

But here's the thing you always need to remember: There's no need to be perfect to inspire others. Instead, inspire people through the way in which you deal with your imperfections. There's not only a lot of value to be found in our imperfections, but from beauty and lessons as well. Our imperfections are what make us unique. They're the driving force behind our ideas and our purpose. And if they can be harnessed properly, the result is often nothing short of magical.

Meet Brian Altriche, the founder of RocoMamas, a local quick service restaurant (QSR) brand that was founded in 2013 and had gone global by 2018. Brian is no stranger to failure. His first franchise left him in debt, he lost almost his entire life's savings on the stock market, he got squeezed out of one business and sued by Red Bull in another. Yet, in each case he's learned and implemented vital lessons that have culminated in the runaway success of South Africa's favourite smart casual phenomenon.

On episode #128 I spoke to Brian about his journey building RocoMamas into a QSR brand and franchise that is poised to take on the likes of global incumbents like Burger King and McDonalds, and what we can learn about value creation in the context of a very imperfect world.

CHAPTER 9 PERFECT IMPERFECTIONS

Despite all category norms and conventions, Brian founded RocoMamas on an imperfect product – a 'smash burger' patty that focuses on taste and experience, which is probably why this 'imperfect' burger has found its place in the hearts and minds of consumers in over a dozen countries around the world (in under five years).

I naturally asked the obvious question: Why found a brand on an imperfect product? I just want to give this some context. If you're familiar with lean startup methodologies, you'll know the value of getting your MVP (minimum viable product) to market as quickly as possible. LinkedIn founder, Reid Hoffman, sums it up perfectly with his famous quote: 'If you're not embarrassed by your first product, you've launched too late.' What he means is that speed to market is more important than perfection. Once you're in the market, testing your product, that's when you can start refining it based on real user feedback.

This is *not* what Brian did. He wasn't trying to launch his brand and then tweak it. He sees the greatness in imperfection. He knows that there's more to a brand and product than cookie-cutter 'sameness'.

'I was grappling with the fact that my two teenage daughters considered fast food normal,' he recounted. 'I hadn't grown up with that. When I lived in the US, I realised you get some fast food that's still made like it was in the 50s. There was a burger place I loved. It was run by a husband and wife team and he smashed the burgers. He used meatballs with no binding agents, and he'd place them on a hot skillet and smash them down. You lose no juices with that method. Everything squeezed out of the meatball is immediately sealed into the patty. Our burger product is completely different to the perfectly manufactured burger patties of the established burger chains. If you have six people eating the same hamburger at one of our tables, every single one of the burgers will look slightly different and this makes each customer feel as though their burger was made especially for them. It's real food served imperfectly.'

This was a deeply personal journey for Brian because he is by nature a perfectionist. 'When I was younger, I used to hunt for perfection and it actually drove me mad. To overcome this, I had to learn to find the beauty in imperfection, so I started delving into different concepts around what beauty is and our obsession with trying to sell something that's perfect. I love excellence and believe that if you're going to build something at scale, you have to be better at something each day than you were the day before. You need to be on a journey of continuous improvement. But that doesn't mean that everything always needs to be perfect.'

Brian's ideas were validated when he opened his first RocoMamas store opposite a McDonalds. 'It was a bit of a protest actually. When we were building the store I even said to the guys, "come on, let's moon McDonalds", and so we did.'

Brian has doubled down on imperfection, right through from the design of the stores themselves, to the way the food is photographed. To this day, all photo shoots take place inside a RocoMamas store. The food is made and served on a table for the shoot. No fake foods are used.

'One photographer we were using suggested that we use mashed potatoes instead of ice cream for one of our desserts. He was concerned that the ice cream would melt. So what? Ice cream melts. Just take the damn photo!'

This idea of an imperfect product being served to customers flies in the face of many conventional business norms, but it's resonating with consumers. Imperfection works today because it builds trust with people who are crying out for authenticity in a world dominated by fake news, misinformation, photoshopped images and Instagram filters.

THE VALUE OF IMPERFECTION

The idea of value being expressed through imperfection dates back thousands of years. Historical records show that magnificent carpets adorned the court of Cyrus the Great, who founded the Persian Empire over 2 500 years ago. The Iranians were among the pioneer carpet weavers of the ancient civilisations, having achieved an unmatched degree of perfection through centuries of creativity and ingenuity.

The skill of carpet weaving was handed down by fathers to their sons, who built upon those skills and in turn handed them down to their offspring as a closely guarded family secret. To give you an idea of the painstaking effort that goes into a Persian carpet, a 9' x 12' Persian rug that has 500 knots per square inch would take four to five artisans working six hours a day, six days a week, approximately 14 months to complete.

And then, after spending more than a year of their lives on one single carpet, these artisans would leave out some stitching to deliberately make the carpet imperfect. This fact had a profound impact on Brian. 'Their cultural belief was that only God can be perfect and therefore nothing man creates should be perfect,' he said. 'By intentionally leaving out stitching they were ensuring that their creations were not perfect. And most of the time, this wasn't even noticed by the average person.'

But here's the really interesting thing about those carpets. Years later (millennia later, really) a study was done where a mass-produced copy of an original Persian carpet with no flaws was hung alongside an original Persian carpet, which did contain missing stitches. People who viewed the carpets were asked which one resonated with them more. 95% of the people who participated in the study chose the imperfect carpet.

I believe that we identify with imperfection because we are imperfect ourselves. Consumers today have finely-tuned bullshit radars and we intuitively know when something is off. If you want your customers to take you seriously, take them seriously. And find the beauty in your imperfections, because they will too.

HOW TO OVERCOME YOUR IMPERFECTIONS

A water bearer had two large pots, one hung on each end of a pole, which he carried across his shoulders. One pot had a crack in it, while the other was perfect and consistently delivered a whole portion of water.

At the end of the long walk from the stream to his house, the cracked pot arrived half full. This continued daily for two years, with the bearer bringing home one and a half pots of water.

The perfect pot was proud of its accomplishments. But the cracked pot was embarrassed by its imperfection, since it fulfilled only a fraction of what it was designed for.

After two years of what it regarded as disappointment, it spoke to the water bearer one day by the river. 'I'm ashamed of myself because this crack in my side causes water to leak all the way back to your house.' The bearer replied, 'Did you notice that there are flowers only on your side of the path, but not on the other pot's side? That's because I've always known about your flaw. I sowed flower seeds on your side of the path and every day on our walk back to the house, you watered them. For two years I've picked these beautiful flowers to decorate the table. Without you being the way you are, I wouldn't have had this beauty to decorate my house.'

What you regard as imperfections and limitations are in many instances good fortune clothed as adversity. Consider Arnold Schwarzenegger's heavy accent when arriving in Hollywood. Not only did his accent not stop him from becoming a Hollywood superstar, it's iconic.

Similarly, Richard Branson's dyslexia did not stop him from establishing his billion-dollar Virgin empire. Sylvester Stallone was once advised his slurred speech would pose an obstacle to him becoming an actor. Even though he wrote the script to the hit film *Rocky*, the producers didn't want him to play the role because of his speech issues. Instead of giving in, Sly channelled those objections into creating a streak of successful films playing the lead character Rocky Balboa, the impoverished boxer hailing from the slums of Philadelphia.

Welcome your imperfections and stop seeing them as an impairment. Your imperfections are intrinsically linked to your potential. Success is only important when measured against one's potential. You can always do more. No matter what Elon Musk achieves in his life, no matter what he does, he'll still think 'I could have done more'. Because we all have the potential to do more. Whether you regret your life and the decisions you make will have a lot to do with how much you did with that potential. And your imperfections are a powerful driving force for achievement.

From an Inner Game perspective, there are two key takeaways. First, it's impossible to reach perfection. Accept that. Don't stop trying, but love the journey, not the destination. Second, if you fixate on your imperfections and overlook your unlimited potential, you will never discover your value. The world rewards value creators. The more value you create, the bigger your reward will be.

CHAPTER 10

Agile entrepreneurship wins the day

Players:	**Pepe Marais** and **Gareth Leck**
	– Founders, Joe Public
Episode:	MBS094
Principle:	*I will zig and zag*

*The voyage of the best ship is a
zigzag line of 100 tacks.*

– RALPH WALDO EMERSON

As entrepreneurs we talk a lot about zigging and zagging, but what we really mean is that we need to be agile. The path changes frequently. It's fraught with obstacles. How you navigate them, and how willing and able you are to adjust to new data, opinions and circumstances will either open up new opportunities for you, or keep you stuck in the past.

The story of Gareth Leck and Pepe Marais is one of the best examples of this that I've had on my show. Their initial idea was to take big agency thinking to the man in the street, under a concept they called 'takeaway advertising'. Their primary mission was to disrupt the advertising space.

Today, their company – Joe Public – is South Africa's largest independent agency, with a turnover of R800 million and gross profits in excess of R250 million. But getting to where they are today was no easy feat. Pepe and Gareth's story includes an exit to a multinational corporate, the repurchase of their company (complete with the contract signed, dated and framed in their office with the plaque, 'Never, ever sell your soul, Joe Public Independence'), losing their biggest client, near bankruptcy and the rebuilding of the company from the ground up on more than one occasion.

My interview with the two founders of Joe Public was particularly poignant for me because it wasn't just about what can go right – it was about everything that can go wrong, but learning to survive anyway. The story of Joe Public is really about the art of zigging and zagging through the hardships and realities of building a scale business – or any business, really.

AN ACT OF GOD

Pepe and Gareth's paths first crossed when Gareth saved Pepe's life. A few years later, they were introduced by a friend who thought they'd make excellent business partners. During their initial meeting, at a local bar in Cape Town called Bardelli, Gareth learned Pepe was a 'boatman' and began recounting the story of how he'd rescued an 'idiot' drowning paddle-skier in April 1995.

Gareth and Greg Bertish, a world-renowned big wave surfer, were surfing the first big storm of the season in Cape Town when Gareth came across a paddle-skier who had clearly had some difficulties. Bleeding from the head and with a broken nose, the boatman was out cold. They were out in the waves but some red rubber piping floated past and Gareth was able to pull the paddle-skier onto the piping and into calm waters where the National Sea Rescue Institute (NSRI) could rescue him. As soon as they had Pepe back on shore the NSRI whisked him away in an ambulance and that was that.

For years, Gareth didn't really think much more about the boatman whom he'd rescued, but never met, and Pepe never knew how he'd ended up lying on red rubber pipes out at sea. But, the longer Gareth spoke, the more Pepe realised that the story sounded eerily familiar. It had to be fate. Gareth and Pepe's business partnership and Joe Public's destiny were sealed.

Joe Public was launched in 1998 as a rebellious creative advertising agency. Gareth and Pepe's first job was for Full House in Cape Town, and they were paid R800 for a logo design. 'We literally danced around the room because we were so impressed that someone would pay us that amount of money for a logo,' Pepe chuckled. For the first six months they didn't earn a salary and were surviving on R1 500 a month from the unemployment insurance fund (UIF). But they didn't care: 'It was so liberating just to be able to get paid to do a job for a company that we owned; we were captured by the ecstasy of making "art as commerce" a reality,' said Gareth. 'We called the business Joe Public because we wanted to make advertising accessible to the man on the street.' Like many startups, for the first few years the partners didn't really have a vision for the company, outside of just working for themselves. But by their second year, they had a safe full of cash and seven figures in the bank. 'Our takeaway advertising play was the definition of zigging while other agencies zagged, and it was working,' said Pepe.

A MAJOR DEAL COMES ALONG

All that zigging and zagging had the desired effect, and business soon picked up, but it also had another unintended consequence – a potential buyer came knocking. 'Our third partner really wanted to sell the business to an international conglomerate that loved our "sexy" takeaway advertising model and, to be honest, the idea of having the option to move to New York was really appealing to me,' Pepe professed.

Ultimately, the deal was made. But it wasn't long before Gareth and Pepe realised that the acquirers didn't want the takeaway model; they only wanted Joe Public's bottom line. The local multinational sold to a larger US-based holding company, and before they knew it, they were just another subsidiary of an international giant.

'We were naive and once we were part of the group, our cost base increased substantially. We were reliant on big projects coming in to cover our costs and as the managing partners, this pressure fell on us. We lost a million rand in one year.'

Looking back, Pepe and Gareth can clearly see that they sold too early and got shafted in the deal. 'But, more than that, we ended up in a corporate environment that was the exact opposite of everything we'd built our business on,' recounted Pepe. 'Our holding company was all about the numbers and it was amazing to see how our creative profile took a dive as a result.'

GETTING ZIGGY WITH IT

During the eight-year period post selling the business, there was a corporate-led merger with another local agency where Pepe, at one stage, made the decision to fire one of the senior executives who came with the merger. It was not an amicable goodbye, and when the exec joined one of Joe Public's biggest clients, he lost no time firing the agency. Since the client accounted for 40% of Joe Public's revenue, all hell broke loose. 'We needed to retrench 50% of our employees. It was devastating.'

But there was an unexpected consequence as well – the value of the business depreciated. 'We realised that for the first time in five years, we had an opportunity to buy our business back. We immediately started negotiating with the holding company. The problem was that they wanted an astronomical amount for the business, which was nowhere near what we'd been paid for it. We didn't have that kind of money. We fought for three years, and eventually resigned. We just said to them, "Take it all. We don't want this." That's when they came back with a reasonable number that we could manage.'

On 26 January 2009, the business partners bought their company back. The day is memorialised in their offices by the aforementioned plaque. With the contract freshly signed and the ink still drying, Pepe and Gareth were celebrating in the car on their way back to the office when they received a call: A media mistake had been made that would cost the company R800 000. Gareth and Pepe had put all their eggs in one basket. They'd leveraged themselves to the hilt to be able to buy back their business. They'd also kept profits and cash flow low since 2006.

'We didn't have R1 million in our bank account and were technically insolvent. Our houses were on the line, our kids were in private school and, to top it all off, it was during the recession, so we lost 30% of our revenue literally overnight,' says Gareth. 'Our revenue was R13 million, but that left very little positive cash flow after salaries and expenses were paid each month and we had no cash reserves. It had been part of our strategy to keep our PE ratio low so that we would be able to buy back the business. We were doing well, winning Loeries and keeping momentum behind the brand, but we weren't chasing profits. We'd never envisioned such a disaster was possible.'

HIPPIE SHIT MAKES BUSINESS SENSE

During this period, Gareth and Pepe focused a lot on their own personal development. Pepe says he had a profound personal insight: 'I learned that I was very self-obsessed about being a great creative, driving a great car, winning awards, being a muso and playing on stage for people and being cool. I had to learn the hard way that none of that was me. As human beings there is a much deeper source within us and that's the thing that I personally began tapping into – being in service of others. This new way of being gave me extraordinary energy. I thought of applying this same purposeful approach to our business and I went in search of uncovering our greater reason for being as an organisation. Once we clarified why our business existed, it completely changed the game for us.'

As a result of this journey, by the time they were able to buy their company back in 2009, Gareth and Pepe had a clear vision of where they wanted the company to go and how they wanted to change course, and it all started with not putting the bottom line first. This is one of the key reasons why they were able to weather almost going insolvent – it wasn't about the money. To this day, Joe Public operates on this principle and has gone on to become one of the most successful advertising groups in Africa because of it.

During our interview, Gareth said that he subscribes to the idea that 'hippie shit makes business sense'. How else can you explain why a business would grow on average by 10% year-on-year for twelve years, and then for the next eight years grow by more than 50% year-on-year? 'You just can't explain how this is possible in a flat industry,' he stated. 'I believe there's something bigger at play now. That's what we discovered.'

FAIL YOUR WAY FORWARD TO SUCCESS

'You need to make mistakes to get the lesson,' says Pepe. 'We needed to reforge the business based on the right culture. To do that, we needed to bring the power of purpose into Joe Public. We feel our purpose on a deep level; it's now the framework of everything we do. We exist to exponentially grow our clients, our people, and our country – in that order. If we focus on clients, we will grow our people, and we will have a good organisation that can positively impact and help the people of South Africa. We call it growth to the power of 'n'.

Revenue growth has naturally followed, but the deeper sense of purpose is helping Pepe and Gareth make a much more meaningful impact. Joe Public registered One School at a Time, a non-profit organisation, in 2008. Through the organisation, they have taken their chosen school in Soweto from one of the poorest performing township schools in Gauteng to within the top three. They raise

R1,2 million a year for the project, of which R250 000 comes directly from Joe Public.

On episode #070, I interviewed Gil Oved, *Shark Tank* investor and the former co-CEO of The Creative Counsel, a local agency that was sold in 2015 for more than R1 billion. We were talking about the inevitable eventualities that will test your will as an entrepreneur. 'Your breakdowns will always be your breakthroughs,' he told me. 'Every time I have felt like it was the end, I've found a way to break through, and every time I kept going it propelled the business forward. You just have to stick with it.'

Just like Gareth and Pepe and the Joe Public story, there will come a time, probably several times, when you will feel like breaking down and throwing in the towel. But I truly believe that no matter how bad things get for you as an entrepreneur there is always another move; something you can do to find perspective on your situation, push through and reach new heights. When I spoke with Howard Mann, the President of Business Brickyard in New York, he told me that you can't read the label when you're stuck in the bottle. It's such a simple idea that at the same time is especially profound. And it's exactly what happened to Gareth and Pepe. They were so caught up in the business itself that they didn't see the huge opportunity of shifting Joe Public away from a profit-focused business, to one driven by purpose and vision.

Building a scale business is hard. It's supposed to be. So, when the proverbial shit hits the fan remember to zig and zag your way through to success. There is always another move. Always. You just need to be agile enough to spot it.

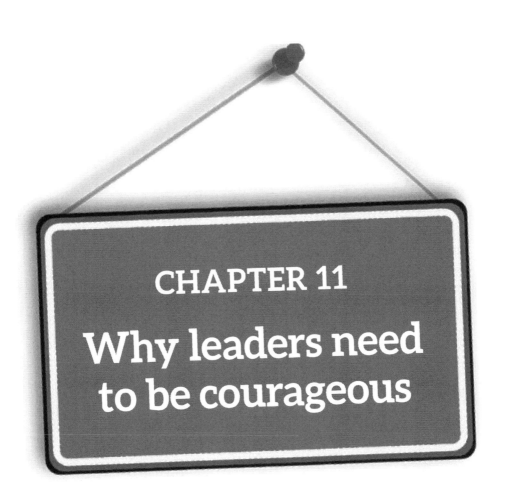

CHAPTER 11

Why leaders need
to be courageous

Player:	**Jonathan Shapiro** aka **Zapiro**
Episode:	MBS126
Principle:	*I will be courageous*

*T*hey say that cartooning is nothing more than organised gossip, but in South Africa, a simple cartoon represents far more than trivial gossip – for Jonathan Shapiro aka Zapiro, cartoons are a commentary on our political and socio-economic reality, and Zapiro's cartoons have been nationwide talking points for over 25 years.

Jonathan has published 27 cartoon books; was the first cartoonist to win a category prize in the CNN African Journalist of the Year Awards; has held solo cartoon exhibitions in New York, London and Frankfurt (and many in South Africa) and, through his running commentary on local political developments has been embraced by Nelson Mandela and Archbishop Emeritus Desmond Tutu.

Jonathan's spark for cartoons happened around the age of four when he became fascinated with the many annual collections of the famous English cartoonist Giles. When he suffered from nightmares, his mother suggested that he draw them as a way to help him overcome his fears.

'We are all cartoonists in a way because when you are three years old you draw whatever's in your head,' he told me. 'It can be rude, unfettered and unhindered by society. Children's drawings are often amazing for this very reason – they even look like cartoons. But as we get older, society pushes us in certain directions and we lose this art. If you can hold onto that head space, if you can remain free to express what you see on your own terms, that for me is a powerful idea,' he said.

This paradigm of using creative expression to communicate and express his world would be prominent throughout Jonathan's life; it would become a tool that would propel

the Zapiro brand onto the world stage and make his political views a household talking point across South Africa.

Jonathan's commentary was first noticed during the
apartheid struggle of South Africa, and he quickly gained
a level of notoriety. It didn't hold him back. Jonathan's
passion for political commentary was largely influenced
by his mother. Just before the Second World War her
family fled Nazi Germany for the United Kingdom, where
his mother survived the Blitz on London. This experience
would leave a lasting influence on the way she thought
about the relationship between courage and truth.

'My mother came to understand something about
persecution – that the saying "never again" doesn't only
mean never again for Jews, but also means never again
for anyone.' The progressive boarding school his mother
attended helped shape her views and she became a
social worker, later doing a course at the London School
of Economics where she met his father, a Cape Town law
graduate who was also studying there. They married
in England and moved to South Africa where she was
confronted with a system of segregation designed to
persecute the black population. Given her beliefs, this
didn't sit well with her and she attempted to become an
activist. 'When she heard about the torch commander
protest group, she joined them on a march and brought my
dad along. My dad's father freaked out, putting a stop to
her activities.' Decades later, in the 80s and 90s, she would
eventually become such a dedicated activist that a Cape
Town ANC branch is named after her.

Meanwhile, as a young mother and frustrated activist, she imparted a lot of what she believed to Jonathan and his siblings. 'From a very young age we were aware that there was evil around us, that we were privileged and things had to change.' The problem was that knowing was one thing – actually doing is another, and Jonathan and his siblings had no clue where to start.

'At university I didn't really do much, apart from some grassroots things like making posters for marches – I had to find banned books in the UCT library to get banned photos of Madiba – but that's not really putting yourself on the line,' he admitted to me. And then he was conscripted to the South African National Defence Force. 'Refusing to go to the army meant a six-year jail sentence and I didn't have the means to flee the country, so I reluctantly went.' It was here that the first sparks of rebellion really took hold. 'I refused to carry a gun and was victimised by the officers. They eventually gave me a lead pole to carry. A really dumb corporal made me stand guard with it. I felt like a walking cartoon.'

In the army Jonathan would very occasionally meet conscripts who'd been involved in the student left – 'guys who knew what it was like to be on the run and be perse-cuted by security police. They kept a low profile. I hadn't experienced that and so I was a bit of a loose cannon, ready to make a statement.'

Halfway through his two-year conscription Jonathan was investigated by military intelligence because he'd got involved with the United Democratic Front (UDF). 'I went to the UDF launch, joined a branch and within a few weeks I was arrested in a motorcade with 14 other activists and locked up in a police station.' They were bailed out by Trevor Manuel, who would later become the first ANC Finance Minister in post-apartheid South Africa. Jonathan stuck it out in the army for the rest of his two years, but during that time he appeared in court several times in his yellow UDF shirt and was found guilty of illegal gathering. He also plastered his naval-base workspace with UDF pamphlets and the 'Free Mandela' sticker that he had designed.

Jonathan's very first artwork for the UDF in 1983 was banned and over the next few years several more of his posters and cartoons were banned. He was cutting his teeth and refining his craft. He was developing lifelong skills that gave headaches to oppressive and corrupt political figures in the apartheid government and would, somewhat ironically, later do the same to corrupt politicians in the new South Africa. Most importantly, he was getting to grips with the consequences of telling the truth about political figures and their wrongdoings in government.

Enter Jacob Zuma, South Africa's president from 2009 until his forced resignation in 2018. Zuma is a frequent feature in Zapiro cartoons.

'One day in 2006 my doorbell rang. I opened the door and standing in front of me was a man in uniform holding some legal papers. I was being sued by Jacob Zuma, for R15 million.' At first, Jonathan just stood there in shock. He couldn't believe it. One of the most powerful politicians in the country had taken offence to three cartoons and was suing a private citizen.

Jonathan's response was priceless, but also proof that courage – like anything – is a muscle that can be worked and developed until it is second nature. 'The very next day, I drew another cartoon of me sitting at my desk with Zuma arriving in my studio. He says, "I'm suing for damage to my reputation." In the cartoon I respond, "Would that be your reputation as a disgraced chauvinistic demagogue who can't control his sexual urges and who thinks a shower prevents Aids?" And I put the three cartoons that he was suing me for back into the cartoon, showing Zuma holding them in his hands.'

Zuma pursued the case even when he became president but after six years dropped the charges. This wasn't the end of the story between them. Zapiro is famous for drawing Zuma with a shower attached to his head as an iconic identifier of some of Zuma's most factually incorrect statements. It became such a big thing that even TV news interpreters for the deaf would make shower mannerisms live on TV whenever Zuma's name was mentioned. In 2008 Zuma again sued Jonathan after he published what is arguably the most famous cartoon of Zuma – the 'Rape of Lady Justice' cartoon. The same court sheriff arrived at Jonathan's gate. When Jonathan saw who he was he said: 'Is that asshole suing me again?' The sheriff couldn't help himself and cracked up. This second lawsuit was widely publicised, both locally and internationally. After four years Zuma again had to drop the charges.

But notoriety does come at a price. There were unforeseen consequences that Jonathan has had to deal with over the years. He's received death threats on a number of occasions and been physically beaten. During the 2010 FIFA World Cup, when South Africa was hosting the tournament, he was attacked while on the fan walk.

'I was identified for some of the cartoons that I had done. A bouncer was sent after me and he smashed me in the face. I thought he'd broken my cheek bone, there was blood everywhere. That was really scary,' he told me. 'But I reckon one of the worst things are lynch mobs on social media. They can take one word or one sentence, or a part of a drawing out of context and can almost destroy you. It's absolutely devastating and is probably the worst thing I have had to contend with.' Despite these challenges, on the strength of his cartoons Zapiro has gone on to speak on world stages in around 20 countries and is one of the world's most respected cartoonists.

HOW TO BE COURAGEOUS

While we may doubt our ability to be courageous, we have no doubt that courageous people change the world. Nelson Mandela's courage changed the political and economic fabric of South Africa. Dr Martin Luther King Jr. used his courage to lead the Civil Rights Movement in America. Sir William Wallace had the courage to lead the First War of Scottish Independence.

Every single successful entrepreneur, CEO, athlete and personality I've interviewed has this principle firmly established as part of their code. Courage is the quality of character that gets them through the pain and hardship 'tax' that everyone has to pay if they are to become great at anything; if they're to become more than what those around them thought was possible. But, being courageous is a choice. If everything you want is on the other side of fear, then you must recognise, too, that the essence of courage is the ability to act in spite of fear. Enter Rosa Parks and her 20 seconds of bravery, whose consequences would span generations to come.

On 1 December 1955, after a long day's work at a Montgomery department store, Rosa Parks boarded the Cleveland Avenue bus for home. She took a seat in the first of several rows designated for 'coloured' passengers. The Montgomery City Code required that all public transportation be segregated and that bus drivers had the 'powers of a police officer of the city while in actual charge of any bus for the purposes of carrying out the provisions' of the code. While operating a bus, drivers were required to provide separate but equal accommodations for white and black passengers by assigning seats. This was accomplished with a line roughly in the middle of the bus separating white passengers in the front of the bus and African-American passengers in the back.

When an African-American passenger boarded the bus, they had to get on at the front to pay their fare, and then get off and reboard the bus at the back door, as they weren't allowed to walk through the 'white' section of the bus either. As the bus Rosa was on continued on its route, it began to fill with white passengers. Eventually, the bus was full and the driver noticed that several white passengers were standing in the aisle. The driver of Rosa's bus stopped the bus and moved the sign separating the two sections back one row, asking four black passengers to give up their seats.

The city's bus ordinances didn't specifically give drivers the authority to demand a passenger give up a seat to anyone, regardless of colour, but Montgomery bus drivers had adopted the custom of moving back the sign separating black and white passengers and, if necessary, asking black passengers to give up their seats to white passengers. If the black passenger protested, the bus driver had the authority to refuse service and could call the police to have them removed.

On that day, three of the other black passengers on Rosa's bus complied with the driver, but Rosa refused, remaining seated instead. The driver demanded she stand up. Rosa's reply? 'I don't think I should have to stand up.' The driver called the police and had her arrested. Later, Rosa recalled that her refusal wasn't because she was physically tired, but because she was tired of giving in to her fear.

She made the choice to act, to stand up against her fear and to stand up for her rights. This simple action was the spark that fuelled the Civil Rights Movement across America.

A MODEL OF LEADERSHIP

All world shapers have their own unique model of leadership, but there is one thing they hold in common: A cause bigger than themselves. Their motivations had nothing to do with their own success, comfort or prestige. Wallace, Mandela and King all fought for the freedom of their oppressed people, as does Zapiro and many others like him. If you examine the code of great leaders throughout history, they didn't thirst for power or success but instead had a cause that addressed moral failures, injustices or even indifferences. If you want to build something that will change the world, you have to start with a cause that is bigger than yourself.

There is another commonality between great leaders: They challenge the status quo. Rosa Parks, Elon Musk, Richard Branson and countless other world-shapers don't accept the views of the people and the world around them. If you're going to grow into an exceptional leader, you have to continually challenge the status quo of both your external and internal environment.

The problem is that courage goes hand in hand with discomfort. It's not easy to challenge the status quo one day, and then expect everything to be smooth sailing the next. But it all starts with you. If you want to change the world – or even a small piece of it – you need to start with yourself. Step one is practising courage. Own your story. Tell the truth about who you are. I've met people who are exceptional at telling their stories, and others who don't know where to start. What I've learned is that we all – and there are no exceptions here – have a story to tell. We just have to believe in it and, more importantly, start sharing it.

ACCIDENTAL BIRTH

Jonathan believes that 'accidental births' are one of the great injustices in the world. 'There are millions of people around the world who are born into dire circumstances. Imagine how many billions of people are kept in those circumstances because they cannot express themselves fully as their situation is just too dire. If you have the opportunity to express yourself, your passions and what makes you tick, you have to have the courage to do it.'

To land his point, Jonathan recounted a conversation he had with Nelson Mandela. He said, 'Madiba, in the four years since I've met you, you would have noticed that my cartoons have become more and more critical of the African National Congress (ANC).' To which Madiba replied: 'Oh, but that is your job. You must do it.' The job in this case was to have the courage to openly express the truth of the ANC as he saw it, through his unique passion for cartoons.

Jonathan's lesson was simple and straightforward. Don't be accidental. Believe that you are here for a reason and that by being courageous, one simple action can lead to a powerful change in your life, business and in the world around you. In life we have many days, but very few moments. You get two types of moments. There are fixed moments, like the day we are born, when we take our first footsteps, get our driver's licence, graduate, get married, have kids and when we die. Then we have fluid moments; moments when you have just a few seconds to choose whether you are going to be courageous or continue to live in fear.

Rosa Parks had one of these moments on the Montgomery City Bus. When she was asked to give up her seat, she had only a few seconds to make her choice. In this moment, the mind has two things going on. First, the brake. This is the part of the brain that tells you not to be courageous and to preserve your safety. The second is the accelerator. This is the part of the brain that tells you that you can be more than what you think you are and to challenge the conventions of society and the status quo.

Herein lies the choice: the brake or the accelerator? Most of us push the brake simply because it's easier to remain safe in the comfort and certainty of what we know, than to face the pain and risk of uncertainty and the consequences of the unknown. Rosa chose to push the accelerator for herself, but that one positive action changed the course of American history.

That is the power of courage and action. Never doubt that in just a matter of a few seconds, one small courageous action can change the trajectory of your life, your business and the world around you.

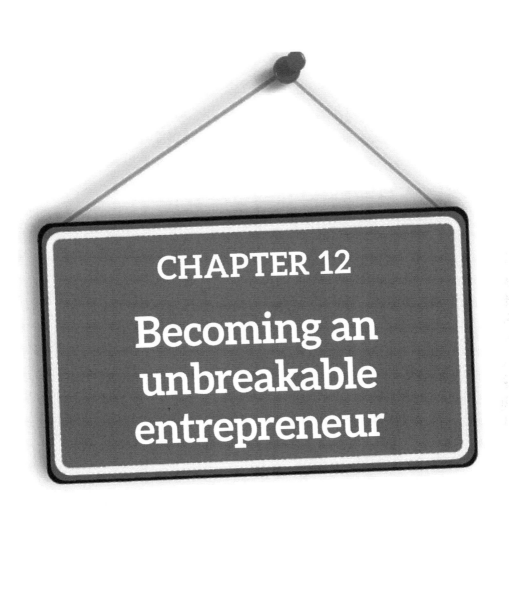

CHAPTER 12

Becoming an unbreakable entrepreneur

Player:	**Rusty Labuschagne**
Episode:	MBS139
Principle:	*I will be unbreakable*

You are only confined by the
walls you build for yourself.

– VÁCLAV HAVEL

*F*ew interviews have affected me as much as meeting Rusty Labuschagne, a man who not only spent ten years in a Zimbabwean prison for crimes he didn't commit, but who isn't bitter about the experience. Meeting him in person, hearing his story and, most importantly, experiencing first-hand his attitude today, gave me my first inkling of what it means to be humble and accept life with grace and fortitude.

Imagine the scene. It's 2003. Zimbabwe is in the throes of President Mugabe's land reform and seizure programmes. Against the backdrop of this tenuous political climate, Rusty is a successful, self-made, businessman running his five safari camps, flies his own aircraft, has nine vehicles, 11 boats, a houseboat, a fishing resort on Lake Kariba and owns a 34-acre property in the city of Bulawayo. Life's pretty good.

But there were some problems, starting with a large amount of fish poaching taking place in the fish breeding grounds near his fishing resort. One day, in response, Rusty and his best friend, Spike, spotted two fish poachers and drove their boat towards them in an attempt to scare them off. The wake caused by Rusty's boat tilted the poachers' boat, causing them to jump into the water. They were about three metres from the shore and soon the poachers scrambled to dry land and ran off into the woods. Rusty and Spike didn't think anything more of it. It was just another day in Africa.

The next day wasn't. When the police arrived, accusing Rusty and Spike of drowning one of the poachers, they couldn't really believe what was happening. They took the police to the scene of the alleged crime and explained what had happened. In response they were asked to report to the local police station, some two hours away, in three days' time. When they arrived at the police station three days later, the first thing they heard over the intercom were the words: 'Have you arrested those two white men yet? This is clearly a murder case.'

STEPPING INTO HELL

That afternoon, Rusty and Spike were locked into a 2m^2 corrugated iron hut in 40-degree heat, without their statements being taken. Two days after denying all charges, Rusty and Spike were transferred to another, larger police station for processing. 'In Zimbabwean police holding cells, it's the same as the prisons, there are no beds. You sleep on the floor. The holding cells are filthy and they stink of faeces, urine and vomit because there are no facilities, only a five litre plastic container, cut off at the top, as a toilet. It was honestly the worst night of my life. The mosquitoes were unimaginable and we were crammed in there like sardines,' recalls Rusty.

Once the news broke of the two arrests 200-plus demonstrators, holding banners, marched towards the prison, calling for the immediate death of the two white men. Rusty and Spike were given bail, pending the trial (which happened 30 months later). At that point, Rusty was advised to leave the country by a politically influential friend, and other close friends, on the basis of inside information and the racial tension in the country.

Rusty decided that he could not leave his family behind, and the thought of being found guilty in the court of public opinion was too much to bear. He didn't run. Instead, he was sentenced to 15 years in jail.

During the trial no evidence was presented of murder – no body, and no statements to that effect by the policemen who attended the scene. And yet the following judgement came through anyway: 'It cannot be said that his aim and object was to kill the deceased. He, in my view, is clearly guilty of murder with constructive intent.' The judge's verdict wasn't the only inconsistency in the trial, but it was the final nail in the coffin.

WHATEVER DOESN'T KILL YOU

I asked Rusty to describe his first day in prison. 'The first thing they do is make you strip naked. You walk in with nothing and I was the only white man amongst 1 000 prisoners, which was unbelievably terrifying given Zimbabwe's political climate and history.

'I was escorted up to my cell, which was 13 metres long by 3 metres wide. There were 78 of us in there. Everybody got 33 centimetres of space, marked out on the walls in chalk. To fit, prisoners had to lay on their sides, with legs all crossing over in the middle. You all faced the same direction and when you needed to turn over, all 78 prisoners had to turn over together. As cushioning against the cold concrete floor, you would fold two of your worn-out, lice-ridden blankets, several times to fit your space, and then you would cover yourself with the third blanket.'

If that wasn't bad enough, it got worse. 'You are also only allowed one set of clothing at any one time and only after six months did you get a change of clothing. Because there were no basins or taps in the cells, we had to wash our clothes in the cell toilet at night, while wearing a blanket. We then had to hang our clothes on the walls, with smuggled book staples, to dry by the next morning.'

'Three or four of us would get together and take turns to wash our clothes, as one garment had to be used to block the toilet to allow the toilet bowl to fill up when attempting to flush. The water only ever dribbled in slowly. Then we would wash the clothes on the cement block surrounding the toilet bowl, dipping them in and out of the toilet as we washed. You have no idea how humiliating it is to wash your clothes in the same toilet that everyone had been using. And yet you did it because the alternative is worse. But the things that hammered me the most were the mosquitoes and the lice, which eat away at you, year after draining year.'

In 2005, while in the notorious Chikurubi Maximum Security Prison, Harare, the capital city of Zimbabwe, ran out of water. For three years each prisoner was only allocated one cup of dirty orange water a day from a local dam. That was to drink, clean your teeth, wash your face, bath, everything. At times prisoners didn't have a bath for nine months at a time.

'During my first six years I watched over 2 200 prisoners die, primarily from malnutrition,' Rusty told me. The prisons were run by ex-military vets and Green Bombers who had been trained to take over local farms. If you stepped out of line, the beatings were severe. 'You'd be put in leg irons, have your hands cuffed behind your back and ordered to lie flat on your stomach. Then you'd be beaten on the soles of your feet with one-metre long rubber batons.' If it doesn't sound that extreme, think again. One hundred hits under each foot. They broke both feet and leg bones.

SURVIVING PRISON: HOW TO BECOME UNBREAKABLE

Rusty served ten years of his 15-year sentence. During that time, he made the decision to survive. It wasn't an immediate decision though.

For a very long time, the only question that occupied Rusty's thoughts, day and night, was 'Why me?' And who can blame him? In Rusty's mind, he had been trying to do the right thing – chasing off poachers near a fishing co-operative – and he'd been crucified for it. That's a tough thing for anyone to accept.

To survive though, Rusty recognised that he needed to get out of his hole. He needed to look at life differently. 'There is no way I could have survived that time of my life if I didn't believe that everything happens for a reason. That's what got me through. There were no answers for all my questions of: Why me? What have I done to deserve this? Am I here to be protected? Do the other inmates feel the same pain or am I different? I had to believe that I was put there for a reason. Once I started thinking like that, I could feel the power that would keep me alive.'

'... and hope. Hope is an incredible thing. If someone had said to me in year one that I was only going home in year three, I would've said never. I was going home now-now. A few weeks or a month I could live with, the thought of more than that was too painful. I had to hold onto the hope that this crazy mess would all be sorted out and I'd be released. I kept my mind positive, no matter what.'

It sounds so simple; but I know the reality must have been anything but. How did Rusty do it? 'It's about finding positives in all the negative things that are happening around you,' he told me. 'Affirmations definitely work. One of my affirmations was "Every day, in every way, I'm getting better and better".'

But hope alone wasn't enough. Rusty had to overcome an immense amount of bitterness and anger. And, it turns out that the biggest lesson Rusty had to learn was about the power of forgiveness. 'I was full of bitterness, anger, hatred, frustration and the need for revenge for what they had done, and were doing, to me. I hated them bitterly and would lie there for hours wishing every terrible thing on each of them in turn – the poacher, the police, the judge, the ministry and all who were involved in my conviction. I remember, after about a year, walking in the exercise yard, tired of all the anger, hatred and bitterness that was draining me daily, and saying: "Lord, take care of them and let me get through this road you have put in front of me." A weight was immediately lifted from my shoulders and I realised, in that moment, that I had accepted my fate. This gave me the mental ability to push the blame aside and stop focusing on what I couldn't control and, instead, focus on my mindset and emotions – two things I *could* control. My whole life in prison changed after that. Most importantly, this gave me the space to forgive. I now know what Nelson Mandela meant by forgiveness, because if you don't forgive you will live in prison forever. You have to let it go. It doesn't matter if it's right or wrong, but if you don't forgive, in the end it will break you.'

Gratitude was another massive lesson for Rusty. 'When you're lying on a concrete floor in your allocated 33 centimetres of space, and the breath you take is no longer your own but that of the person lying next to you, gratitude begins to take on an entirely new meaning. I looked back on my life with new eyes. I'd been unbelievably lucky up until that point. I'd been given beautiful children, great opportunities and material gains. Instead of focusing on the fact that I'd lost everything, I chose instead to be grateful that I'd had those things at all. Most of the men I spent each day with had never had those opportunities. In prison I realised how, despite having so much, I hadn't really been happy – I could never buy enough. It was always about more, more, more and in the end there was never enough. That's not what life's about. It's really about making a positive difference to the people around you.'

I've spoken a lot about regret in this book and, of course, I needed to know if Rusty has any regrets. Had he made the right choice on that day he decided to chase those two poachers? 'I wouldn't change a thing,' he told me. 'I couldn't see it at the time, but there was a bigger picture at play for me. Before I was arrested, I thought I was bulletproof; flying high like a big fish in a little pond, going nowhere.

Now I'm a small fish in a big pond, making a huge differ-ence in many people's lives. I feel I finally have a purpose. I was always motivated by material things, but this experi-ence has taught me that that's not what life is about. Life is about making a difference and having a clear purpose.'

THERE ARE NO BREAKTHROUGHS WITHOUT WALLS

Perhaps the most glaringly obvious lesson from my perspective was this: If you want to build a business, there's literally nothing stopping you, aside from the walls you've built around yourself. It's a great irony to think that both Rusty and Nelson Mandela found peace as a result of being in prison. Not every man or woman walks out of prison with that level of insight, or at peace with them-selves and the world. It's incredibly difficult to find peace when things go wrong: Sickness, insolvency, divorce, job loss and poverty. These things can all crush us. It's easy to start blaming others, or things outside of your control, for your own circumstances. But putting blame at the feet of everyone or everything else will get you nowhere. The most successful individuals I've met, from Joey Evans to Rusty Labuschagne, have an incredible ability to put their lives into perspective. They're able to understand that the trajectory of your life really is up to you.

I believe there are two types of entrepreneurs in this world: Those who live in cause, and those who live in effect. 'Cause' entrepreneurs tend to be in control of their own destiny. They're victors, not because bad things don't happen, but because they overcome whatever life throws at them.

'Effect' entrepreneurs are always the victims – victims of circumstance, bad luck, market pressures, aggressive competitors – the list goes on. They're at the mercy of the whims of the world around them. If you want to build something of purpose – whether it's a good business, a great life, or both, you need to start getting real with yourself. Stop accepting self-imposed boundaries. Stop putting up walls around you. You will never break through a wall of self-taught lies about who you are and what you're capable of if you're living in 'effect'.

It took me a long time to understand those walls. They're glass, so we generally don't see them. It's pretty much Howard Mann's point about living in glass bottles again. We create a myopic world view for ourselves. I wanted to understand how those walls got there though and, after a lot of thought (and triangulation), I realised that we spend our whole lives unconsciously building them, brick by brick, each time something goes wrong, or we fear the outcome of a specific situation.

The only way to break through them is to accept the reality of things for what they are; more than that, we need to believe that things can and will improve with the right mindset and attitude. Change is possible.

This is what Rusty did, but there are far more – and less extreme – examples all around us. Building a business is tough. Leading a life of purpose that is successful and makes you happy is tough. Neither will happen by accident. It takes deliberate focus, patience and practise.

Each entrepreneur needs to learn how to sow the seeds of becoming unbreakable. First, by understanding that the negative and self-doubting stories we keep telling ourselves about how things are going to be, what the past means and what the future holds, are all bullshit. Only you have the power to control and shape your destiny. Bad stuff might happen along the way – you will fail, you'll make mistakes, you'll cry. That's okay. Just don't let any of those things break you. We're in control of the walls we build for ourselves and we're also in control of the meaning we will find in breaking them down, brick by brick.

For the full story of Rusty's incarceration and lessons learned I highly recommend his book *Beating Chains*.

*A*s I write this conclusion, I'm sitting in London at the London Tech Week conference. We're here because Digital Kungfu won the Best Tech Startup in Africa award at the Africa Tech Week 2019 Awards.

Africa Tech Week is a partnership between the Department of International Trade, London Partners and UK-SA Tech Hub, which means that as one of the winners we were invited to attend this global showcase of technology, startups and entrepreneurship.

It's surreal that the personal journey I've been on while writing this book has culminated in this place, at this time, mingling with some of the most innovative technology startups in the world.

When I look back at my own journey, it's abundantly clear to me that if I hadn't codified how I approach business and entrepreneurship through a clear set of Inner Game principles, that I wouldn't be here today.

None of our success at Digital Kungfu would have been possible because I would still have been trying to find my purpose. These principles really do work. They've worked for me and countless other entrepreneurs whom I've interviewed, and I believe that they can work for you too.

But let me leave you with the single biggest learning that most entrepreneurs and 'ideas' men and women face at one point or another: Theory without execution is worthless.

I entreat you to not only apply these principles in your life, but to hold yourself accountable to them as well. See them through. Tell someone else what you're doing –

whether it's a partner, mentor or friend – and ask them to check up on you.

Remember that you are never alone. Every challenge that you're currently facing (or will face) in your business has been overcome by someone else in their business. You just need to ask for help. I mean it. Fuck your pride and ask for it. When you do, doors that were once closed will open.

The dominant theme at the London Tech Week conference has been exponential technologies like Artificial Intelligence (AI), additive manufacturing, advanced robotics, virtual and augmented reality, robotics, alternative energy systems, biotechnology, and digital medicine – it truly is the most exciting time in our history to be an entrepreneur, whether you're in these industries, or will benefit from them.

This only tells half the story. These technologies promise to unlock market opportunities for entrepreneurs on a never-before-seen scale.

But here's the catch – these same opportunities will only be secured if your Inner Game, aka your decision-making operating system, is built on a solid foundation and a set of principles that will push you to persevere when everyone else is telling you to quit; that looks to the future and is willing to be agile and open to new ways of doing things and new ways of thinking; to be certain of who you are and what you want to achieve in a world of uncertainty; and to be unbreakable in the pursuit of your dreams.

It's time to tell *your* story...

STAY IN TOUCH WITH MATT BROWN

Website:
https://mattbrownshow.com

Twitter:
https://twitter.com/mattbrownza

LinkedIn:
https://www.linkedin.com/in/mattbrownza/

YouTube:
https://www.youtube.com/channel/UCSJJaWxrug2ECnRWG1y9fyw

Facebook:
https://www.facebook.com/mattbrownza/

Instagram:
https://www.instagram.com/mattbrownza/

SoundCloud:
https://soundcloud.com/matt-brown-show

Printed in Great Britain
by Amazon